DATE DUE

DE 5 '97			
AP 30			

DEMCO 38-296

The Kingdom of Saudi Arabia

The Kingdom of Saudi Arabia

DAVID E. LONG

University Press of Florida

Gainesville/Tallahassee/Tampa/Boca Raton

Pensacola/Orlando/Miami/Jacksonville

02 01 00 99 98 97 C 6 5 4 3 2 1

02 01 00 99 98 97 P 6 5 4 3 2 1

Library of Congress Cataloging-in-Publication Data
Long, David E.
The Kingdom of Saudi Arabia / David E. Long.
p. cm.
Includes bibliographical references (p.   ) and index.
ISBN 0-8130-1471-9 (c : alk. paper). — ISBN 0-8130-1473-5 (p : alk. paper)
1. Saudi Arabia.
DS204.L65   1997
953.8—dc21   96-45618

The University Press of Florida is the scholarly publishing agency for the State University System of Florida, comprised of Florida A & M University, Florida Atlantic University, Florida International University, Florida State University, University of Central Florida, University of Florida,
University of North Florida, University of South Florida, and University of West Florida.

University Press of Florida
15 Northwest 15th Street
Gainesville, FL 32611

To my wife, Barbara,

and to Virginia and Jack

Contents

Maps, Tables, and Figures

PREFACE

When viewed through Western eyes, Saudi Arabia presents many anomalies. It is a barren land endowed with huge oil wealth; its affluent society places more importance on lineage and blood ties than on personal wealth; and its government is devoted to both rapid modernization and the preservation of an Islamic way of life that is 1,400 years old. Seeking to understand these anomalies is in many ways more of an absorptive process than an analytical one. Facts are important (if sometimes hard to come by), but it is the feel of the place that leads to real understanding. And getting a feel for Saudi Arabia is probably the most elusive task for foreign resident and reader alike.

There is, of course, no substitute for firsthand experience in gaining a feel for the kingdom, but even residence does not necessarily confer understanding. Thousands of Western business executives, technocrats, government servants, and their families have resided in the kingdom for periods of years; yet a surprising number of them have never really seen what is around them, and many return home with the same misperceptions they came with or absorbed from equally unperceptive expatriates already living in the country.

This book is aimed primarily at the nonexpert or at least the reader whose principal area of expertise is relatively narrow—for example, oil, national security, business, economics, or politics. It is an attempt to portray Saudi Arabia as more than a compilation of facts and figures. Indeed, those who seek insight through statistics might do better to look elsewhere. Not only are statistics often unreliable in this part of the world, but even reliable statistics by themselves do not adequately portray what the country is all about.

I do not wish simply to emphasize seeing the problems and challenges with which Saudis are wrestling; I also wish to emphasize seeing those problems through Saudi eyes to the greatest extent possible. For a Western observer to try to communicate to a primarily Western audience what Saudis perceive is both presumptuous and perhaps ultimately impossible. Nevertheless, for such an important country—the greatest repository of oil in a world that increasingly requires oil imports—it is better to see through a glass darkly than not to see through it at all.

In general, I have used a standard scholarly transliteration system, with occasional variations, usually in names—following the spelling preferences of people or organizations—or in quoted material.

It is impossible to acknowledge all the people who had a hand in producing this study, but I would be remiss if I did not mention a few. The book is in many ways a culmination of personal insights and experiences as well as considerable research since early January 1967, when I first landed at the Jiddah airport with my wife, Barbara, to take up my new position as a junior political officer at the American embassy. My greatest debt of gratitude is to her for her faith and support over all those years as well as for her relentless vigilance as my chief editor and critic.

The first person I met in Jiddah was my new boss, Bob Stookey, from whom I learned far more about the kingdom than I can say. Soon thereafter I met Ambassador Hermann Eilts, who has remained a major inspiration as I have sought a better understanding of the country and its inhabitants. He assigned me my first report on the annual Hajj, which later became the core of a book and the basis of the chapter on the Hajj in this one. During that first tour in Jiddah, I also met St. John Armitage at the British embassy, who over the years has kindly allowed me to benefit from his long experience and keen insights.

Back in Washington several years later, I worked for Phil Stoddard and the late Herbert Liebesny, and to both I owe an eternal debt for the standards of analysis and writing and editing skills they instilled in me. Both encouraged me to finish my graduate studies (the Hajj book was my dissertation) during which I took a tutorial from Herb on Islamic law that in fact lasted until he retired from government service several years later. My doctoral advisor was Bernard Reich, who has been a close friend and colleague ever since. I cannot begin to express what I owe to Bernie. Without his pushing me, I might never have finished this book.

I am also indebted to the Council on Foreign Relations for granting me a fellowship (more than likely, I believe, because Alton Frye got me mixed up with another candidate) and to the Center for Strategic and International Studies (CSIS), where I spent my fellowship year studying the Gulf. While at CSIS, I met Jack Bridges, one of the most dynamic people I have ever known, and together we explored the role of Saudi Arabia in the energy crisis years of the 1970s. Working for him was Virginia Forbes, who has ever been a source of quiet inspiration.

I also got to know many Saudis, including Prince Turki Al Faysal, who has helped me enormously in researching various studies on the kingdom, and Prince Bandar bin Sultan, for whom I was a teacher (although I could never decide who taught whom the most). It was also at that time that I began a long and rewarding friendship with Saeed Badeeb, who more than anyone else has enabled me to gain an understanding of Saudi Arabia and the Saudis.

Another person to whom I am grateful is Governor John West, who, as U.S. ambassador to Saudi Arabia in the Carter years, provided me with invaluable opportunities to roam about the kingdom learning as much as I could. His deputy was Jim Placke, from whom I still seek counsel on oil matters and who advised me on the oil and economics chapters of this book. During that period, I collaborated with Jack Shaw on another monograph on Saudi Arabia, beginning another lasting friendship and gaining an invaluable advisor and critic.

I also thank Bob Oakley and Ben FitzGerald for their always-insightful advice as well as David Rehfuss, formerly senior economist with the Riyad Bank, whose suggestions were invaluable on economic matters and whose tables appear in the chapter on economics. In addition, I thank Lucia Rawls and David Mack, who read parts of the manuscript; Wayne Neill and Vahan Zanoyan, who with Jim Placke tutored me on Saudi oil; Khalid Bubshait and David Bosch of Saudi Aramco, Fred Dutton, and Abd al-Rahman al-Shaia of the Saudi Information Office in Washington, all of whom helped me obtain photos for the book; and General Ahmad al-ʿAnaizi and Prince Abdallah bin Faysal bin Turki Al Saud, who offered valuable comments. Thanks also to Mike Schmidt, who kept my computer running, and Jennifer Stowe, who did a great job on the graphics. To all these people and many more I send my sincerest thanks.

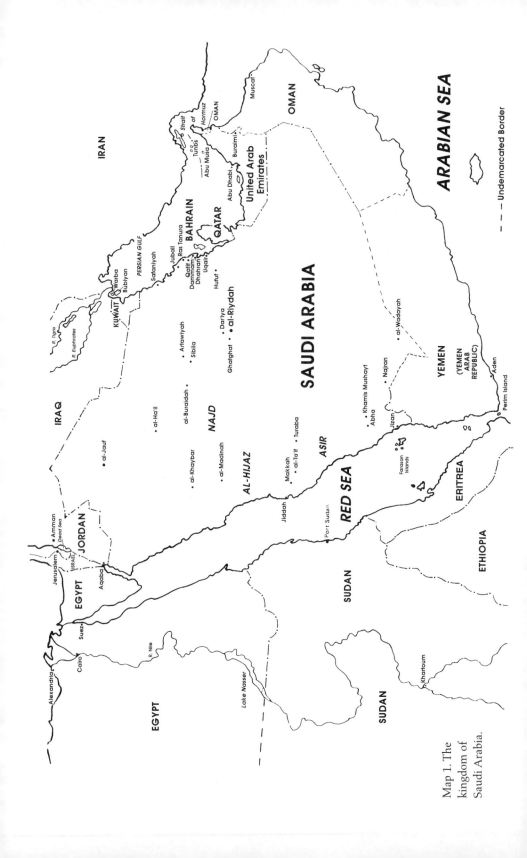

Map 1. The kingdom of Saudi Arabia.

1

The Land and the People

Saudi Arabia is a country of startling contrasts—a huge land mass and a small population; a barren desert terrain situated over great oil wealth; a traditional Islamic society undergoing rapid modernization; a closed society that is often in the news. Although these contrasts have evoked a good deal of fascination with the country, they have also helped to create misleading stereotypes and exacerbate the problem of understanding the country and its people.

The Saudis themselves have not made the problem any easier. Products of a closed society, they tend to keep outsiders at arm's length; and it is difficult to develop personal relationships beyond a superficial social or professional level. People who have dealt with Saudis for years can be as surprised as the casual observer by their reactions to events. Nonetheless, by seeking to look behind the stereotypes, one can glimpse the Saudis as they really are—a deeply religious, traditionally conservative, proud people who have been forced to make the transition from the pre-industrial to the modern age in less than two generations.

The image of what Saudi Arabia is really like is often in the eye of the beholder. For example, most of the world is overwhelmingly interested in Saudi oil. Under the country's arid surface lie roughly 260 billion barrels of oil, about one-quarter of the world's proved oil reserves; and most of it is available for export. Although it is not an overstatement to say that the developed world cannot maintain its current standard of living without Saudi oil, it is a gross overstatement to say that Saudi social values and political expectations are inextricably based on oil production. Saudi society is thoroughly Islamic and oriented to the extended family; bloodlines are ultimately more important than oil wealth.

Saudi Arabia is also an Arab state and has thus been drawn into Arab world politics, including the Arab-Israeli dispute. In this context, the kingdom has been willing to initiate punitive measures when it believes they have been appropriate (as the 1973–74 Arab oil embargo demonstrated), but it prefers quiet diplomacy in the search for peace. Both quiet diplomacy and punitive measures have in the past earned the kingdom criticism from abroad—the former by militant Arabs, who believed that the kingdom should have adopted more confrontational policies against Israel and its supporters; the latter by Israel's supporters, who condemned all opposition to Israel and often saw the "Saudi oil weapon" lurking behind Arab policies against Israel. Ironically, all parties to the dispute apparently took it for granted that the kingdom would bear the lion's share of the huge financial costs attendant on any practical Middle East peace settlement. When this assumption appeared erroneous after the 1993 Israeli-Palestinian Agreement demonstrated the need to fund the new Palestinian political entity, the kingdom received even more criticism from abroad.

With so much attention given to oil and Middle East politics, few Westerners are aware that to the Muslim world (one-fifth of the world's population) the kingdom is more important as the location of the two holiest places in Islam—Makkah and al-Madinah.[1] Performing the annual Hajj, or Great Pilgrimage to Makkah, is an obligation for all able Muslims once in their lifetimes. Attended each year by roughly 2.5 million of the faithful, it is not only one of the world's greatest religious celebrations but one of the greatest exercises in public administration. The Saudi government is responsible for ensuring that all those who attend get through the event without serious injury and with a minimum of discomfort. Because the Hajj occurs annually in Saudi Arabia, fully occupying the entire resources of the Saudi government for almost two months each year, I will devote a separate chapter to this unique event.

In short, despite the internal contradictions that make generalizing so difficult, the key to understanding the kingdom is to view it on its own terms, not on the basis of why it is important to the outside world. The place to examine first is the environment that has shaped the attitudes and values of Saudi society, and then look at the people themselves.

The Land

Physically, Saudi Arabia occupies about 2.25 million square kilometers (865,000 square miles), making it between one-fourth and one-third the size of the continental United States. Because many of its boundaries are still undefined, the exact size cannot be precisely determined. The borders with Yemen and Oman are not yet fully demarcated, although the kingdom has agreed in principle to borders with Oman and plans to negotiate the border with Yemen. The borders with Jordan, Iraq, and Kuwait, however, are demarcated. The Saudi-Kuwaiti neutral zone and a Saudi-Iraqi neutral zone, created in 1922 to avoid tribal border hostilities, were abolished in 1966 and 1975 respectively and their territories divided among the parties. The decades-old Buraymi oasis territorial dispute among Saudi Arabia, Oman, and Abu Dhabi was settled in 1974 when Saudi Arabia agreed to give up its claim to the oasis and adjacent territory for an outlet to the Persian Gulf through Abu Dhabi.

Occupying about 80 percent of the Arabian peninsula, Saudi Arabia abuts the Red Sea in the southwest and the Gulf in the northeast. It is bounded by Jordan to the northwest; Iraq and Kuwait to the north; Bahrain (offshore), Qatar, the United Arab Emirates, and Oman to the east; and Yemen to the south. Traditionally, land borders were relatively meaningless to Saudi rulers, who looked on sovereignty more in terms of tribal allegiance. Tribal areas were huge and only vaguely demarcated because the tribes themselves followed the rains from waterhole to waterhole and wandered over broad areas. In the 1920s, the British, as mandatory power of Transjordan and Iraq and protecting power of Kuwait, pressured the Saudi government to accept land borders with all three countries. Later, when oil became so important in the region, the borders acquired much more importance. A deviation of a few centimeters from a common point could translate into hundreds of square kilometers when projected for long distances over the desert. Thus, the discovery of oil in disputed areas has made negotiation of the remaining undemarcated borders all the more difficult.

The same can be said for offshore territorial limits. Saudi Arabia claims a twelve-nautical-mile limit offshore as well as a number of islands in the Gulf and the Red Sea. With extensive oil discoveries in the Gulf, it became imperative to establish a median line between Saudi Arabia and Iran. Not until the 1970s was the line finally negotiated, however, following a number of provocative incidents involving Arabian American Oil Company (Aramco) offshore oil rigs and the Iranian navy.

Early European geographers delineated the Arabian peninsula into two parts. Arabia Felix, or Fertile Arabia, had as its locus the relatively well watered highlands of Yemen in the south and the adjoining mountains of 'Asir and the Hijaz. The rest of the peninsula was called Arabia Deserta, or Desert Arabia. Thus, except for the western highlands, most of Saudi Arabia is desert interspersed with oases, some lying along the banks of *wadis* (intermittent-stream riverbeds) and others covering huge areas such as al-Hasa in the east.

With a predominantly desert terrain, a shortage of water is one of Saudi Arabia's main resource problems. In the interior are nonrenewable aquifers that are being tapped at an unprecedented rate, particularly as urbanization and population expand and agricultural development projects are created. To augment water supplies, the kingdom has created a massive water desalination system.

Despite its arid climate, sporadic rains do fall in Saudi Arabia and occasional snow in the mountains. This water has to run off somewhere; and as a

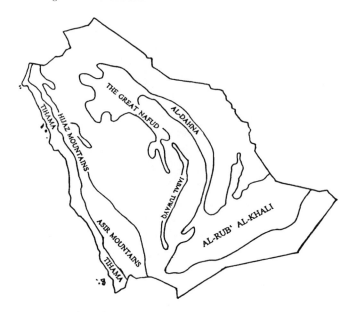

Map 2. Topographical features of Saudi Arabia.

result, there are numerous drainage systems made up of intersecting wadis. After local and occasionally heavy rains, the wadis can become rushing torrents. In the 1960s, a European construction company building a road in central Arabia did not construct adequate bridges to take sufficient account of potential water flows. When the rains came, huge stretches of road washed out. The final indignity occurred when the company's main field camp was also flooded out. By contrast, the builders of the now-defunct Hijaz railroad, which took pilgrims south from Damascus to al-Madinah before World War I, suffered no such lack of foresight. One can still see sturdy stone bridges along the abandoned rail bed spanning open desert. Among the major wadi drainage systems in the kingdom are Wadi Sirhan, located on the Saudi-Jordanian frontier; Wadi al-Batin, which flows northeast toward Kuwait; Wadi Rimah, which flows eastward from the northern Hijaz mountains; and Wadi Dawasir and Wadi Bishah, which flow eastward from the southern Hijaz ('Asir) mountains.

While nearly all of Saudi Arabia is arid, only part of it consists of real sand desert. There are three such deserts in the kingdom. The Nafud, sometimes called the Great Nafud, is located in the north (*nafud* is one of several Arabic words meaning "desert"); the Rub' al-Khali, literally the Empty Quarter, stretches along the entire southern frontier; and the Dahna, a long, narrow area, curves in a great arc from the Nafud westward and then south until it joins the Rub' al-Khali. The sand in all three deserts contains iron oxide, giving it a pink color that can turn to deep red in the setting sun.

The Rub' al-Khali, covering more than 550,000 square kilometers, is the

Figure 1. Saudi Aramco exploration buggy, Rubʿ al-Khali. Photo by Saudi Aramco.

largest quartz sand desert in the world. (The few local tribes call the area *al-rumal*, "the sands.") It is also one of the most forbidding and was virtually unexplored until after the 1950s, when Aramco teams began searching for oil in the region.[2] Much of the Rubʿ al-Khali is hard-packed sand and salt flats, from which sand mountains rise as high as three hundred meters. In places, these giant dunes form long, parallel ridges that extend for up to forty kilometers (twenty-five miles). Most of the area is uninhabited, and the Arabic dialects of those few people who live there are barely intelligible to Arabs living outside the area.

The Nafud, about 55,000 square kilometers, is made up of slightly smaller sand ridges (reaching about ninety meters in elevation) divided by flats that can extend up to fifteen kilometers in width. Winter rains, when and where they happen to fall, can make these valleys lush grazing areas in the spring.

Geographically, the kingdom is divided into five areas. In addition to the Empty Quarter, there are central, western, eastern, and northern regions.

Central Saudi Arabia

Central Arabia, or Najd, is both the geographical and the political heartland of the country. It was here that Muhammad Ibn Saud, amir of a tiny oasis principality, Darʿiya, joined the Islamic revival movement of Muhammad ibn Abd al-Wahhab, subsequently called Wahhabism, and laid the original groundwork

Figure 2. Dar'iyah from the Wadi Hanifah.

for the creation of the Saudi state. Najd extends westward to the Hijaz mountains, south to the Rub' al-Khali, north to the Nafud, and east to the Dahna. Running through the center for about six hundred kilometers and roughly parallel to the Dahna is Jabal Tuwaiq, a westward-facing escarpment rising 100–250 meters.

Najd, which means "highlands" in Arabic, consists mainly of sedimentary plateaus interspersed with sand deserts and low, isolated mountain ranges. The most prominent range is Jabal Shammar in the north. Until the 1920s, the Shammar tribes were under the leadership of the Al Rashids of Ha'il, political rivals of the Al Sauds during the late nineteenth and early twentieth centuries.

Many cities and towns are scattered throughout Najd—the largest, of course, being the national capital, al-Riyadh, on the Wadi Hanifa. Riyadh is the plural of *rawdha*, Arabic for "garden," and was so named for the number of vegetable gardens and date groves located there. From a small oasis town of about 7,500 at the turn of the century, it has grown into a major metropolis with a population approaching 2 million today.[3]

Riyadh has changed incredibly in the last forty years. My first sight of the capital was in January 1967, in the company of an American engineer who had last seen it in 1948 when it was still essentially a mud-brick city. The engineer could not recognize anything until he got to the central square in the

Figure 3. Entrance to King Abd al-Aziz's palace, Riyadh, 1937. Photo by Saudi Aramco.

middle of town. The city had grown by then to 200,000 people, and many of the old mud-brick houses had been torn down and replaced by drab concrete structures built by Egyptian and other Middle Eastern contractors.

Riyadh in the 1960s was still virtually closed to Westerners, who numbered only about three hundred. In King Abd al-Aziz's lifetime, diplomats making the long trek to Riyadh for a royal audience were required to wear local Arab dress when calling at his traditional mud-brick place, the Murabbʻa Palace. With the oil boom of the 1970s, however, the city was opened up; and by 1975, the Western population numbered more than 100,000. Since then, the changes in the physical appearance of the capital have been even more startling. New buildings are constructed as fast as old ones can be torn down, and what was formerly open desert has become suburbs and shopping centers. The pace of growth has been so rapid that the ruins of Darʻiya, the ancestral home of the Al Sauds some eighteen kilometers north of Riyadh, is now a virtual suburb.

Development is not limited to Riyadh. To the northeast, between Riyadh and Haʼil, is the district of al-Qasim, with its neighboring and rival cities of ʻUnayza and Burayda. The people of al-Qasim are among the most conserva-

Figure 4. Riyadh after a rare rainstorm, 1968.

Figure 5. Modern Riyadh at night. Photo by Information Office, Royal Embassy of Saudi Arabia.

tive in the kingdom. At the same time, modernization projects have changed the face of these and other provincial towns as much as they have Riyadh. Moreover, Qasim has become the breadbasket of Saudi Arabia due to heavy public and private investment in modern, large-scale irrigated farming. The main problem arising from investment in large-scale agriculture is environmental concern about water resources currently supplied by unreplenishable aquifers.

Western Saudi Arabia

The hinterland along the Red Sea coast can be divided into two topographical areas—a flat, arid, but humid coastal plain known as Tihama and an escarpment chain of mountains. The coastal plain narrows considerably north of Yanbuʿ, and in the far north the escarpment extends almost to the sea. The western face of the mountains drops off precipitously, particularly in the south, and the few roads climbing it wind their way past remnants of even steeper camel trails that used to be the only way to the top.

Figure 6. Modern road from Makkah to Taʿif, 1969.

Figure 7. Rural scene in ʿAsir, 1969.

The mountains are divided into two ranges. In the north, they do not exceed 2,000 meters (6,400 feet) and are generally much lower as one travels south. Just north of Taʾif, they pick up again, gaining in elevation as they approach the Yemen border. These are the Hijaz mountains. The highest point in the kingdom is Jabal Suda (Black Mountain) near Abha, which exceeds 3,000 meters. The kingdom has built a national park along its crest.

On the eastern side of the escarpment, the mountains fall off gradually toward the Najdi plateau and, farther south, toward the Rubʿ al-Khali. On the eastern side of the mountains there are a number of huge lava fields (*harrat*) where the terrain looks like a lunar landscape. The largest, Harrat Khaybar, is just north of al-Madinah.

Western Saudi Arabia was historically divided into two principalities: the Hijaz, which extended from what is now the Jordanian border to just south of Jiddah, Makkah, and Taʾif; and ʿAsir, to the south. ʿAsir (the term means "difficult" or "dangerous" in Arabic) was quasi-independent until the Saudi conquest in the 1920s and 1930s and remained relatively isolated until modern roads were built in the 1970s.

Topographically, this mountainous area resembles Yemen more than it does the rest of the kingdom. There are trees and flowing streams and distinctive fortresslike stone houses with decorative whitewash painting. Green terraced fields cling to steep mountainsides. The main urban areas are al-Jizan, a modest city on the coast; Abha, the provincial capital, atop the escarpment; and Najran, inland on the Saudi-Yemeni border. Not far from Abha is Khamis Mushayt, site of a major Saudi military cantonment. The Hijaz (*hijaz* means "barrier" or "boundary" in Arabic) was a separate political entity until it was conquered by King Abd al-Aziz in 1925; and then as now, its life revolved around Islam. Within the region are located the holiest cities in Islam, Makkah and al-Madinah. One of the five basic pillars (tenets) of Islam is the Hajj, or Great Pilgrimage to Makkah. Every Muslim must at one time in his or her lifetime make the Hajj if physically and financially able to do so. While on the Hajj, most pilgrims also visit al-Madinah, where the Prophet Muhammad lived for a portion of his life.

Since the beginning of Islam in the seventh century A.D., an extensive service industry has grown up to cater to Hajjis. It has traditionally been the backbone of the Hijazi economy and, before the discovery of oil, was the basis of the entire Saudi economy as well. With more than 2 million (2.5 million in 1994) attending each year, most of whom stay in the Hijaz for two to five weeks, the Hajj is a major economic and commercial as well as religious event. Physical infrastructure to accommodate the Hajjis is extensive, including one of the largest commercial airports in the world at Jiddah, the traditional port of entry.

Makkah and al-Madinah are forbidden to non-Muslims. With the presence of Muslims from all over the world, however, they possess a cosmopolitan atmosphere that could rival any major city in the world. The Saudi government has spent billions of riyals upgrading the holy sites in both cities, in part to accommodate the ever-increasing number of Hajjis.

Jiddah, on the Red Sea coast, has grown from a small port noted for its multistoried, Turkish-style houses decorated with wood carvings and latticework to a bustling, modern city of more than 1 million people, replete with skyscrapers, urban renewal, and city beautification. When King Abd al-Aziz first incorporated the Hijaz under his rule, he kept many national government agencies in Jiddah, including the Ministry of Foreign Affairs and all the embassies, preferring to protect Riyadh from contamination by the secularizing influences of Western society. Jiddah lost some of its status in the 1970s when Riyadh was opened up to Westerners and eclipsed Jiddah as the economic and diplomatic center of the country. But with the Hajj and a long tradition of Hajj trade, Jiddah remains the commercial hub, and its mercantile mentality is readily apparent.

Left: Figure 8. Old Jiddah, 1967.
Below: Figure 9. Modern Jiddah. Photo by Saudi Aramco.

Eastern Saudi Arabia

Historically, the most important populated area in the east was al-Hasa oasis. Al-Hasa, or its variant al-Ahsa, means "sandy ground with water close to the surface."[4] The term aptly describes the area between the Dahna and the Gulf coast, the area now designated by the Saudis as the Eastern Province.

Immediately east of the Dahna is the Summan plateau, a barren, wind-blown area of ancient watercourses and occasional mountains. East of the plateau is a broad, flat, gravelly coastal plain that extends to an irregular coastline marked by numerous *sabkhas*, or salt flats. Sand hills are dispersed throughout the plain, expanding into the Jafura, a small sand desert that joins the Rub' al-Khali in the south.

Al-Hasa oasis, located inland from the coast, is the largest oasis in the world; and its major town, al-Hufuf, is both an agricultural center and a residence for oil field workers. A smaller oasis, al-Qatif (and its principal town of the same name), is located to the north on the Gulf coast. The two oases are home to the majority of Saudi Arabia's Shi'a community, many of whom, particularly from Qatif, have found employment with Aramco since the earliest days of the company.

The primary significance of the region is that underneath it lies the bulk of Saudi Arabia's huge oil reserves. The Ghawar field, which stretches for more than two hundred kilometers north to south, is the largest single oil field in

Figure 10. Moat and walls around old Hufuf, 1935. Photo by Saudi Aramco.

Figure 11. Old Customs House, Ras Tanura, 1935. Photo by Saudi Aramco.

the world. The economy of the Eastern Province is predominantly oil-based, and even recent efforts to diversify the industrial base focus on petrochemical industries.

The capital and principal city of the province is Dammam, just south of al-Qatif. Once a small pearling and privateering port, it is now a bustling metropolis. South of Dammam is Dhahran, whose name is far more familiar in the West. It is actually not a city but the location of Saudi Aramco headquarters, King Faysal University, the American Consulate General, and Dhahran International Airport. Nearby, on the coast, is al-Khubar, which grew from virtually nothing to an important industrial service city.

Located along the coast north of Dammam to the Kuwaiti border are a number of oil facilities, beginning with Ras Tanura, the principal Saudi Aramco oil terminal, and extending to Khafji in what was once part of the Saudi-Kuwaiti Neutral Zone until it was abolished in 1966. Just north of Ras Tanura is al-Jubayl, the site of the first disembarkation of American oil men, who waded ashore in 1933 to what was then a small village. Today it is the site of much of Saudi Arabia's petrochemical industry and the Saudi navy's principal Gulf naval base, all constructed within the last twenty years. South of Dhahran is the small town of 'Uqayr. Largely overlooked by recent development, it was at one time, with al-Qatif and al-Jubayl, a principal port for trade with Najd and the site of several early political meetings between King Abd al-Aziz and the British.

Northern Saudi Arabia

The area extending along the kingdom's northern frontiers with Jordan and Iraq is physically isolated from the rest of the country by the Nafud. It is geographically part of the Syrian desert; and the tribes in the area claim kinship with fellow tribes in neighboring Jordan, Iraq, and Syria, occasionally owning passports from all three countries. In the northernmost part of the country, the Wadi Sirhan forms a great depression, extending southward from Jordan. It was the traditional caravan route for traders from the Fertile Crescent traveling to central and eastern Arabia.

There are no cities in the region. The two principal towns are al-Jawf and Sakaka, located in oases just north of the Nafud. Before the 1967 Arab-Israeli war, the most important installation in the region economically was the Trans-Arabian Pipeline (Tapline), which carried crude oil from the Eastern Province to the Lebanese port of Sidon. With that route closed due to Israeli occupation in southern Syria (the Golan Heights), Tapline has lost much of its economic importance, although oil is still sent through the pipeline to Jordan.

Climate

Saudi Arabia has the harsh, hot climate that one associates with a desert area. There are variations, however. In the interior, the lack of humidity causes daytime temperatures to rise sharply, and readings can register more than 54 degrees C (130 degrees F). The same lack of humidity also causes temperatures to drop precipitously after the sun goes down, sometimes as much as 20 degrees C (70 degrees F) in less than three hours. Subfreezing temperatures are common in winter, and the ever-present winds create a wind chill that can be very cold for those not properly dressed.

The coastal areas combine heat and high humidity. The humidity usually keeps the temperature from exceeding about 40 degrees C in the summer but likewise prevents it from dropping more than a few degrees at night. Thus, both summer days and nights are steamy and unpleasant. Winter temperatures, on the other hand, are warmer and balmier at night than they are in the interior, particularly along the Red Sea. Along the coasts and in the interior, rainfall is very sporadic. Torrential rains can flood one area while entirely missing areas a few kilometers away. At other times, the same area can go without rain for five to ten years. The sporadic nature of the rains is why desert pastoralists must cover wide areas in search of pasture for their livestock.

The mountain areas are cooler, particularly in 'Asir, where it can get quite cold at night. The 'Asir also gets the moisture-laden monsoon winds from the south in the winter, when most of its annual rainfall falls (about five hundred millimeters).

THE PEOPLE

Official Saudi census figures placed the population at 16.9 million in December 1992, of which 12.3 million were Saudis and 4.6 million foreigners.[5] Due to the large number of nomads and social resistance to efforts to count the number of women, these figures seem somewhat high. Rayed Krimly suggests a range of 7 to 8.5 million Saudi nationals in 1990, based on five different statistical projections.[6] My estimate is 14 to 16 million, of which about 4 to 5 million are expatriates.

Although the population is relatively small in comparison to the country's great wealth, official Saudi estimates show that it is growing at about 3.7 percent a year, one of the highest rates in the world. Unless it begins to level out, the kingdom may face a major socioeconomic problem in the next century as more and more young Saudis chase fewer and fewer jobs. Increasing numbers of unemployed or underemployed young people—while their basic needs are being met by their families—are beginning to feel marginalized, frustrated, and resentful of the establishment, not for what it does but because they are not a part of it. It is such people who become willing listeners to the militant political message of the radical Islamists.

The indigenous Saudi population is among the most homogeneous in the Middle East. Virtually all Saudis are Arab and Muslim. Of course, this fact is not surprising when one considers that the Arabian peninsula is the cradle of both Arabism and Islam. The only non-Muslims are expatriates who are in the country either doing business on contract or representing home governments; they are not permanent residents. Bloodlines, not geography, determine nationality; and being born in Saudi Arabia does not automatically entitle a person to citizenship.

The importance of bloodlines is a manifestation of the basically tribal nature of Saudi society. Tribal in this context refers to genealogy, not to occupation or politics. The days when the tribes were an independent political force have long gone, their power forever broken by King Abd al-Aziz. Even before modern urbanization, Saudi political power emanated mainly from sturdy yeomen villagers in Najd, not from nomads; but the villagers also had tribal affiliations.

The extended family rather than the clan or tribe is the most important social institution in Saudi Arabia. If put to the test, loyalty to one's extended family would probably even exceed loyalty to the state. After all, the state has been in existence for a few decades, and most Saudis trace their families back for centuries. Extended families often live together in the major cities in large family compounds. With the high cost of real estate, however, and as each succeeding generation brings more nuclear families, that practice is becoming increasingly difficult to maintain.

Saudi family dynamics are still overwhelmingly traditional and contrast sharply with practices based on contemporary Western social values. This is particularly so in gender relations. Much has been written in the Western popular press about the inferior role of women in Saudi society, and indeed many younger women find many traditional social practices oppressive. These practices should be viewed from their proper perspective, however, and not simply from that of Western values. In the traditional Islamic Saudi family, men control business and public affairs while women control the home. (Women can own their own property, however, and manage it as they wish.)

There are few areas of the world where women are as domineering in the home as Saudi women are. On family decisions, they tend to present a solid front that men dare not ignore with impunity. There is generally a matriarch—a grandmother or mother-in-law—who rules the home with iron control, and not even her sons care to thwart her wishes. For example, the mother of King Fahd during her lifetime expected and received daily visits from her sons when they were in town, no matter how busy their schedules. And it is the matriarch rather than the husband who imposes the most onerous restrictions on a young wife.

The trade-off for women's power inside the home is virtually no mobility to pursue outside interests. There is almost no contact between the sexes in public, where women must be veiled and are not even allowed to drive automobiles. Job opportunities for women are very scarce and restricted to a few areas where they deal only with other women. Given the prevalence of traditional social values in the kingdom at present, most Saudi women would probably not be willing to sacrifice their control inside the home for greater mobility; but how long this attitude will predominate is an open question, particularly with over half the population under fifteen years old and a growing number of women receiving higher education. Moreover, young men are increasingly supportive of more mobility for women, if for no other reason than economics. For example, with rapid population growth and declining economic opportunities, the expense of hiring a driver to take the women out while the men are at work is becoming a growing burden for younger families. There appears to be no desire, even among the most modernized Saudi women, to abandon traditional Islamic social values; but within the traditional social framework, significant change in what is considered acceptable behavior for women seems only a matter of time.

With genealogy so important, there is relatively little social mobility in Saudi Arabia. Najd is not only the center of Saudi political power, but its tribal affiliations are among the most aristocratic in the Arabian peninsula. Members of the leading tribal families of Najd are at the top of the social order and nontribal families and descendants of former slaves near the bottom. This does not mean that members of the latter classes cannot rise to positions of power. The finance minister under King Saud, Muhammad Surrur Sabban, was from a former slave family, yet he became one of the wealthiest and most influential men in the kingdom.

Historically, slavery in Arabia, although certainly a violation of human rights, was never the inhumane institution that it was in the West. Slaves, even though they were owned by their masters, still had more status, derived from their owners, than nontribal people did, and their owners had the responsibility of caring for their welfare. When Prince Faysal, then acting as prime minister, formally abolished slavery in 1962, many slaves, particularly of the royal family, refused to go. One ex-slave told me some years later, when I asked if he served the king: "I am no servant; I am a slave!"

The population of the Hijaz is far more cosmopolitan than Najd, due to centuries of immigration connected with the Hajj. The leading families formed a merchant class that grew up in the Hijaz to serve the Hajj. Their origins were far more varied than those of Najdis, with fewer tribal affiliations, although many could trace their lineage as far back as Najdis could. The Hadhrami community is an example of nonindigenous residents in the Hijaz. Most of them came to the Hijaz from the Wadi Hadhramout in the southern part of Yemen within the past one hundred years, although some go back much further.

With the concentration of the oil industry in the Eastern Province, that area has developed a polyglot population that equals the Hijaz's. Many of the pre-oil families had close family ties to other Gulf states, particularly Bahrain. The Qusaybi (Gosaibi) family, for example, has a large branch in Bahrain as well as in the Eastern Province.

The Eastern Province is the home of the only significant minority in the kingdom, the Shi'a community, which numbers between 500,000 and 600,000. They live mainly in al-Qatif oasis on the Gulf coast and inland in al-Hasa oasis. Unlike much of the population, Shi'as are willing to work with their hands and over the years have become the backbone of the skilled and semi-skilled oil industry work force. Under Aramco, discrimination by the Sunni majority was greatly mitigated.

Uninterested in inter-Arab politics during the tumultuous 1960s, the Shi'as were considered excellent security risks for sensitive technical jobs. With the Iranian revolution in 1979, however, concern increased that they could become a fifth column for the revolutionary Shi'a politics of Iran, undermining security in the Eastern Province. Of particular concern was the younger generation, which took for granted the social and economic gains Aramco had given their fathers and grandfathers. The younger generation apparently sparked the disturbances in November 1979 and the riots in February 1980. Iranian propaganda in Arabic is beamed at the Shi'a community from Radio Tehran and Radio Ahwaz and is a regular topic of conversation in the Husayniyas, Shi'a religious study centers that are a major feature of Shi'a social life as well.

To date, fears about the loyalty of the Shi'a community have not been realized. Not only did the government belatedly invest more money in infrastructure in Shi'a areas, but the Shi'a community itself proved highly suspicious of the revolutionary regime in Tehran. Thus, they perceived the Iran-Iraq war as an Arab-Persian conflict more than a Sunni-Shi'a conflict. From their perspective, they are Arabs, not Persians; and while they might be second-class Saudi citizens, they still have attained a level of prosperity that they would not wish to give up for the harsh, theocratic rule they see in Iran, even with the remote possibility that such a regime could be carved out of predominantly Sunni Saudi Arabia.

A few families of non-Arabian origin have also become Saudi nationals. Most are found in the Hijaz and are descended from Hajjis who never returned to their homelands after the pilgrimage. Some of these families have lived in Jiddah and Makkah for centuries and have attained stature in society and high rank in government, mainly associated with the Hajj.

Others, of more recent vintage, have eked out a living as unskilled laborers. At the time when Abd al-Aziz conquered the Hijaz, thousands of these people lived around Jiddah in cardboard villages. Some would stay only long enough to earn enough money to begin their return home, mainly to Africa; others were more or less permanent residents. Over time, the Saudi regime tightened its entry and resident requirements and repatriated most of these Hajji laborers.

An interesting group of non-Arabs that have become Saudi nationals are the central Asian community, often collectively called "Tashkandis," "Turkistanis," or "Bukharis" after areas and cities in former Soviet central Asia. They are descendants of a group of political refugees who escaped overland from the Soviet Union in the 1920s. Fiercely anti-Communist and devoutly Muslim, the community took refuge in several countries before finally ending up in Saudi Arabia. Because of their faith, loyalty, and disinterest in inter-Arab politics, many of them were accepted into the Saudi military and security services.

Another group of naturalized Saudis are the descendants of a remarkable group of non-Saudi Arabs who came to Saudi Arabia for various reasons in the 1930s and stayed on as senior advisors. These included Rashad Pharaoun, a Syrian who originally came to serve as the personal physician to King Abd al-Aziz and remained to become a senior advisor; Yusif Yassin, a Syrian who became deputy foreign minister under Prince (later King) Faysal; and Hafiz al-Wahba, an Egyptian who also became a senior advisor.

The distinction between "foreigners" and "natives" breaks down somewhat when looking at neighboring states—for example, the Hadhrami community in the Hijaz and the Eastern Province families with ties in other Gulf states. Indeed, many of the old Sunni families of Kuwait and Bahrain migrated from Najd some three hundred years ago. Northern Saudis have close tribal ties in Jordan, Syria, and Iraq. All these ties are reflected during the Hajj, when members of the Gulf Cooperation Council (GCC) states are not required to obtain Hajj visas. No matter how long one's family has resided in the country, however, one is still identified by the family's original place of origin.

The expatriate community, numbering about 4 to 5 million, comprises between one-fourth and one-third of the total population. Before the oil boom of the 1970s, the Eastern Province probably had the largest concentration of expatriates because that is where the oil industry is located. At one time, Aramco employed literally thousands of expatriates.

Most of the rest of the expatriates were historically located in the Hijaz, then the economic and diplomatic center of the country. When Riyadh was opened up to development in the 1970s, it became the largest city in the kingdom and now probably contains the most expatriates.

The largest number of expatriates in Saudi Arabia are from nearby Middle Eastern countries, South Asia, and the Philippines and are mainly skilled and unskilled laborers and service industry personnel. Despite relatively harsh living conditions, there is virtually an unending supply of menial foreign labor. Economic opportunity is still much greater than at home, and in many cases working conditions at home are equally harsh or harsher. The Yemeni community was formerly the largest, estimated as high as 1 million. Its numbers were drastically reduced following Operation Desert Storm, both for security reasons and in retaliation for Yemen's political sympathies toward Saddam Hussein. At present, however, Yemeni workers are again being allowed into the kingdom.

The status of Western executives and technicians is much higher. Nevertheless, isolation from a generally closed Saudi society, puritanical social norms, and the lack of physical mobility (particularly for women) make family life for Westerners who are used to more permissive societies difficult despite high salaries.

There has been speculation about how much foreign workers pose a threat to the regime through the spread of liberal political and social ideas. In fact, their political and social impact on Saudi society appears to be slight. There is virtually no social contact between Saudis and skilled and semiskilled workers, and the closed nature of Saudi society makes contact with white-collar, mostly Western expatriates minimal also. Moreover, foreign workers of all classes are in the kingdom primarily to make money and then return home, not to make political converts.

There are some exceptions to the lack of social interaction between Saudis and foreigners. The large numbers of public school teachers imported in past years, particularly from Syria and Egypt, have served as a conduit for spreading militant Islamic political teachings, even though foreign teachers are now increasingly being replaced by Saudis. Perhaps a greater potential danger to internal stability, however, is the economic frustration of a growing number of expatriates who have experienced late or deferred payments for services rendered, spurred by Saudi financial problems.

How long the traditional patterns of Saudi society remain entrenched is an open question. Saudi society, which was at a pre-industrial level just a few decades ago, is rushing into modernity at an unbelievable pace. The impact of development on the society is everywhere present. Urbanization is bringing people to the cities, where they are cut off from the support systems of traditional society. Modern communications and transportation have brought the world to the doorstep of what had long been one of the most remote and isolated countries on earth. The evolution of Riyadh into the economic as well as political hub of the country has brought Saudis from all over the kingdom and foreign workers and professionals from all over the world, making it a highly cosmopolitan city. It is not uncommon for families to have several houses scattered over the kingdom, reflecting job, government, and place of origin.

The miracle is not how much Saudi society has changed; it would be inconceivable to assume that great changes had not occurred. What is really extraordinary is how resilient the society has been in the face of change. The family system is still intact and indeed is probably the most stabilizing force in the country. Whatever Saudi Arabia's political or economic future, it is difficult to visualize without the paramount importance of family ties.

2

Historical Background

Western scholarship on Saudi Arabia is a relatively recent phenomenon. While some of it is very good, little of it adequately conveys a sense of historical tradition. Personal accounts of early Western travelers to Arabia are often a better way to get a feel for the history of the country before it was cluttered up with fast-food restaurants, 747s, and other Western contributions to world culture. These travelers included Sir Richard Burton, who wrote a fascinating nineteenth-century account of sneaking into Makkah during the Hajj; Charles Doughty, whose prose evokes the image of an Old Testament prophet; and the prolific H. St. John B. Philby, who first came to Arabia during World War I. If one reads Arabic, the great eighteenth- and nineteenth-century Najdi chroniclers such as Husayn Ibn Ghanim and 'Uthman Ibn Bishr are another source of historical tradition.[1] Although they lack Western standards of historiography, they convey a true sense of the timelessness of culture and conflict behind the rapid, indeed breathtaking, pace of modernization during the past quarter-century.

Two strains of tradition are inseparably bound to the political history of Saudi Arabia: family and religion. As I noted in chapter 1, family tradition is as old as Arabia itself. Religious tradition dates to the founding of Islam. The two came together in the mid-eighteenth century in the persons of Muhammad ibn Saud and Muhammad ibn Abd al-Wahhab. Muhammad ibn Saud (*ibn* means "son of" in Arabic) was the founder of the Al Saud, or House of Saud, the royal family of Saudi Arabia. Muhammad ibn Abd al-Wahhab was the founder of what is widely known as the Wahhabi revival movement. His descendants are the second most prestigious family in Saudi Arabia after the royal family and are called the Al al-Shaykh, or House of the Shaykh. (The surname comes from the fact that Muhammad ibn Abd al-Wahhab was called "the Teacher," or the *Shaykh* in Arabic.)[2] The fusing of temporal power represented by the Al Saud and spiritual power represented by the Al al-Shaykh has sustained Saudi political cohesion from that time to the present.

Muhammad ibn Abd al-Wahhab and His Revival Movement

Muhammad ibn Abd al-Wahhab was born in 1703/4 in 'Uyayna, a small oasis town on the Wadi Hanifa in Najd. His father, Abd al-Wahhab ibn Sulayman, was himself a noted scholar and a follower of the then largely forgotten Hanbali school of Sunni Islamic jurisprudence. Hanbali law was to become the basis of his son's revival movement. The family was a member of the Bani Sinan tribe, which had been in central Arabia since antiquity.[3]

Muhammad was something of a child prodigy, memorizing the entire Quran by the age of ten. He married at twelve and settled down early to a life of scholarship. Central Arabia may have been physically isolated in those days, but not intellectually. Muhammad not only absorbed ideas from the outside Islamic world but, in his younger years, traveled in pursuit of his studies. He performed the Hajj to Makkah, going on to al-Madinah, and also traveled to Basra, Baghdad, and Damascus. In al-Hasa oasis, he studied under Shaykh Abdallah ibn Ibrahim al-Najdi, a noted scholar who later moved to al-Madinah, where he became known as al-Madani.

Muhammad ibn Abd al-Wahhab returned to his native 'Uyayna around 1744 and began preaching against the lax behavior of the townspeople and their disregard for Islamic law. His preaching formed the basis of the puritanical Islamic revival movement that was later called Wahhabism. At the heart of the revival was the Islamic doctrine of *Tawhid* (strict monotheism), and the adherents of the revival called themselves *Muwahhidin*, or "unitarians." To this day, many of the followers of the revival take offense at the being called Wahhabis. The term, first applied by the movement's detractors, was believed by the followers themselves to denote the deification of the movement's founder and is thus a desecration of the sovereignty of God.

The revival is firmly rooted in Sunni Islamic law; and although Shaykh Muhammad rejected the supremacy of any single Sunni school of Islamic jurisprudence, he based his revival on Hanbali law, the most conservative in personal law of the four recognized Sunni schools. (The others are Hanafi, Maliki, and Shafa'i, all named after their respective founders.) In particular, the revival was influenced by the writings of an early Hanbali reformer, Taqi al-Din Ahmad ibn Taymiyya (1262–1328).

Shaykh Muhammad condemned innovations (*bida,* or false practices that had crept into Islam over the centuries), calling them polytheistic. He particularly decried a common practice of the time: venerating noted holy men and making pilgrimages to their tombs, usually domed structures whose custodians often profited from the resulting religious tourism. To this day, Saudis, including the royal family, bury their dead in unmarked graves lest the tomb of some revered family member become a holy shrine.

Muhammad ibn Abd al-Wahhab's uncompromising puritanism was not popular in ʿUyayna, and he was quickly expelled from his native town. Forced to seek another place from which to preach his revival, he soon found himself in the nearby town of Darʿiya and was invited to stay by the local amir, Muhammad ibn Saud, who had become a convert. Thus began the collaboration between spiritual and temporal powers that has lasted to this day. Muhammad ibn Abd al-Wahhab died in Darʿiya in 1792.

MUHAMMAD IBN SAUD AND THE CREATION OF THE FIRST SAUDI STATE

Genealogy is very important in Arabia. Bloodlines are generally traced back, fictitiously or otherwise, to two quasi-mythical figures thought to be the original Arabs—Qahtan, whose descendants generally (although not inevitably) settled in southern Arabia, and Adnan, whose descendants settled in northern Arabia. The Al Saud traces its ancestry to Bakr ibn Waʾil ibn Rabiʿa ibn Nazar ibn Maʿad ibn Adnan. The family reportedly moved from al-Qatif oasis in eastern Arabia to Najd in about 1450.

The founder of the royal house, Muhammad ibn Saud ibn Muqrin ibn Markhan, was born about 1703/4. By the time he met Muhammad ibn Abd al-Wahhab in 1744, he had been for two years the amir of Darʿiya, a petty principality just down the Wadi Hanifa from ʿUyayna. The revival movement that he embraced quickly attracted other converts, many of whom were desert warriors; and under the banner of Tawhid, they began to convert the Najdi tribes and transform the traditional and constant condition of Bedouin warfare into a holy crusade. For the rest of his reign, Amir Muhammad constantly engaged in warfare. By the time he died in 1765, most of Najd had come under his rule, including ʿUyayna, where Muhammad Abd al-Wahhab personally chose the governor to succeed ʿUthman, the ruler who had exiled him. ʿUthman was put to death by followers of the new revival movement.

So long as military expansion was limited to central Arabia, it went largely unnoticed by the outside world. But under Muhammad ibn Saud's son, Abd al-Aziz (1719/20–1803), and his grandson, Saud (died 1814), Muwahhidin warriors ranged far beyond Najd, and the family domains were expanded to include most of the Arabian peninsula. In 1801, the Muwahhidin sacked the town of Karbala, a Shiʿa holy city in what is now southern Iraq. They destroyed the large domed tombs of various Shiʿa holy men, including the tomb of the Prophet Muhammad's grandson, Husayn, one of the most venerated of all Shiʿa "saints." Indeed, Shiʿas consider Karbala and the tomb of Husayn to be the third holiest site in Islam after Makkah and al-Madinah. Two years later, in 1803, the Al Sauds captured Makkah from the Hashimites, descendants of the Prophet Muhammad who had ruled in Makkah for centuries and were then under the suzerainty of the Ottoman sultans. The Al Sauds were forced to withdraw from the Hijaz when plague decimated their army, but they retook it in 1806. They allowed the Hashimite ruler, Sharif Ghalib, to remain as governor.

To the east, the Muwahhidin pushed all the way to Oman, where they forced the Omani sultan to pay tribute. As the revival movement gained adherents in the Gulf, Muwahhidin privateers began sailing out with increasing zeal to prey on the merchant shipping of unbelievers. Privateering was not merely profitable; from their viewpoint, they had a religious duty to oppose evil by attacking the shipping of non-Muslim unbelievers and non-Muwahhidin Muslim "heretics"—a sort of religious bounty hunting. The British, however, who had become the principal Western maritime power in the region and were forced to defend the sea-lanes to their empire in India, considered the Muwahhidin to be pirates. Thus, the Gulf littoral that is now part of the United Arab Emirates earned the sobriquet "the Pirate Coast."

In a relatively short period of about sixty years, the Saudi regime had been transformed from a tiny oasis principality to an important Middle Eastern state. It is interesting to speculate on what might have happened if the Sauds had possessed the military technology to match their military zeal. Just this mixture of courage and fanaticism must have enabled the original armies of Islam to topple empires and expand all the way from Spain to Indonesia.

Such an event was not to happen a second time, however. The Saudi capture of the Muslim holy places was not only seen as an affront by the Ottoman caliphate, but it also deprived the Ottomans of considerable revenues. They asked the ruler of Egypt, Muhammad Ali, who was technically the Ottoman viceroy, to recover the Hijaz and invade Najd. Muhammad Ali harbored his own territorial ambitions in Arabia and in 1811 dispatched an army under his son, Tusun. After several years of fighting, the Egyptians finally retook the Hijaz with the holy cities of Makkah and al-Madinah but were not able to subjugate the Muwahhidin. Then in 1814 Amir Saud died, and his son, Abdallah ibn Saud (reigning 1814–18), retreated to the Najdi heartland.

In 1816, Muhammad Ali sent a second son, Ibrahim Pasha, with a well-equipped army to invade Najd. After two years, Ibrahim entered what was left of Dar'iya, and the first Saudi state came to an end. Abdallah ibn Saud was sent in exile to Cairo and later to Constantinople, where he was beheaded. Dar'iya was totally destroyed, its palm groves cut down and burned. It never recovered, and its ruins can still be seen about twenty kilometers north of Riyadh.

In the Gulf, Muwahhidin privateers were left to fend for themselves. The British had already sent several expeditions to the lower Gulf to put down the pirates but had failed. In December 1818, a large British naval and land force assembled at Ras al-Khaymah, a small principality on the Pirate Coast. The

Figure 12. The ruins of Dar'iyah, the first Saudi capital. Photo by Saudi Aramco.

British were finally able to defeat the local Muwahhidin forces, and in 1820 the local amirs agreed to a truce banning privateering. The agreement also created the basis for British hegemony in what became known as the Trucial States. British protection lasted until 1971, when these small principalities formed the United Arab Emirates.

THE RISE AND FALL OF THE SECOND SAUDI STATE

Although the destruction of Dar'iya seemed to herald the end of the Al Saud as a political force in Najd, such was not the case. In 1824, Abdallah's great uncle, Turki ibn Abdallah (reigning 1824–34), again assembled an army of tribal warriors under the banner of Tawhid and drove the Egyptian garrisons from Najd. He did not return to Dar'iya, however, but established himself at Riyadh, which has remained the Saudi capital to this day.

The birth, fall, and rebirth of the Saudi state began a pattern that was to continue down to the reign of the present king's father, King Abd al-Aziz. After a period of territorial expansion, internecine rivalries within the family would undermine the regime, and outsiders would seize power; then, after a time, a new Saudi leader would appear to repair the family fortunes and re-gain its patrimony. The process began again in 1834 with the assassination of Amir Turki by a member of a collateral branch of the family, Mishari ibn Abd al-Rahman. Turki's son, Faysal, defeated the usurper and succeeded his father. In 1838, however, the Egyptians again invaded Najd, captured Faysal, and brought him back into exile for a second time to Cairo. (Faysal had been among the original exiles in 1818.) Muhammad Ali, who still had ambitions to extend his hegemony over the Arabian peninsula, placed Faysal's cousin, Khalid ibn Saud, in his stead as amir of Najd. Khalid, a younger brother of the executed Abdallah, had also been exiled to Cairo in 1818 and was still residing there.

Khalid reigned as a virtual Egyptian puppet until 1840, when other foreign political reverses forced Muhammad Ali to withdraw his troops from Najd. The following year, Khalid was ousted by Abdallah ibn Thunayan, who replaced him as amir. Abdallah was descended from Thunayan, a brother of Muhammad ibn Saud, and the founder of the Thunayan branch of the royal family.

In 1843 Faysal, who had escaped from Cairo, returned to Riyadh, where he displaced Abdallah and again became amir. Faysal's second reign (1843–65) was to be the zenith of the Saudi state in the nineteenth century. Faysal and succeeding Saudi amirs were more often addressed as Imam than Amir. Amir is a secular title—the head of an amirate. Imam has a religious connotation. In this context, it means the leader of the *Umma,* or the Muslim community (that is, the "nation"). The term can also be used for the prayer leader in a mosque, a Muslim political leader, or (in Shi'a Islam) the leader of all Islam (that is, the "Hidden Imam").

The late historian R. Bayly Winder described Faysal, who adopted the religious title, as "farsighted enough to realize that he could not convert the whole world to Wahhabism, and that if he tried he would again bring ruin on his people and himself. . . . He was a devout Wahhabi, but, instead of attacking Karbala, he received a British diplomat (Col. Lewis Pelly) in his capital."[4]

During Faysal's long reign, he restored order to Najd and expanded his domains north to the Jabal Shammar region and south to the frontier of Oman. He restored Saudi control over the Buraymi oasis, which the Saudis continued to claim although they again lost it in the late nineteenth century. The situation evolved into a major border dispute that was not settled until 1974.

Faysal's brother, Jaluwi, who was a loyal lieutenant, became the founder of another collateral branch of the family, the Ibn Jaluwis. For many years Ibn Jaluwis governed the Eastern Province of Saudi Arabia, and a number of Bint Jaluwis (*bint* is the female equivlent of *bin* or *ibn*) have married into the current ruling branch of the family.

Faysal's death in 1865 heralded another decline in Saudi fortunes. Two of his sons, Abdallah and Saud, were bitter rivals and constantly engaged in civil war. Abdallah was imam from 1865 to 1871, when he was ousted by Saud. Foolishly requesting help from the Ottomans, who had reoccupied the Hijaz after the death of Muhammad Ali in 1844, Abdallah was imprisoned by them for a few months, escaped to reclaim power, and was finally ousted again by Saud. After Saud's death in 1875, a third brother, Abd al-Rahman, claimed power but was ousted by Abdallah, who again became imam. When Abdallah died in 1889, he was succeeded by Abd al-Rahman.

While the Al Saud brothers were fighting among themselves, the state that Imam Faysal had restored began once more to collapse. In 1871, the Ottomans reoccupied al-Hasa in the east. In the south, Oman and the Trucial States (with British assistance) shook off Saudi rule; and in the north, Jabal Shammar revolted. Muhammad ibn Rashid, amir of the Shammar, had served Imam Faysal as governor in the north from the Rashidi capital at Ha'il. By the time Abd al-Rahman became imam, Muhammad ibn Rashid controlled nearly all of Najd and soon forced Abd al-Rahman to be his governor in Riyadh. After an unsuccessful attempt to challenge Rashidi hegemony in 1891, Abd al-Rahman fled in exile with his family to Kuwait, bringing the second Saudi state to an end.

Abd al-Aziz "Ibn Saud" and the Creation of Saudi Arabia

From humiliating defeat and exile, the Al Sauds reemerged stronger than ever to create the third Saudi state, the present-day Kingdom of Saudi Arabia. The story of this extraordinary feat is largely the story of one man—Abd al-Rahman's son, Abd al-Aziz ibn Abd al-Rahman Al Saud, known throughout the world as Ibn Saud.[5]

Abd al-Aziz (1880–1951) was an imposing figure of a man, well over six feet tall, handsome, with a commanding presence that caused other men naturally to gravitate to his leadership. What really set him apart from his contemporaries, however, was his breadth of vision—that innate ability to look beyond the immediate problems facing him and contemplate a future that his background and education did not really enable him fully to grasp. During his long political career, he successfully dealt with neighboring rulers, Western diplomats, and oil executives alike. Although he did not live long enough to see his work reach ultimate fruition, he not only re-created the Saudi state but began the process that was to transform that state into the modern oil kingdom that is Saudi Arabia today.

The process of re-creating the Saudi state was not the irresistible tide of success that it might appear to be nearly a century later. In the words of Philby, it was "the drama of a cause slowly but surely proceeding to its climax of final success through various vicissitudes of fortune, which now propelled it comet-like to the zenith, and now flung it headlong into the depths from which recovery seemed well nigh impossible."[6]

The first step in this process was to recapture the family capital of Riyadh from the Al Rashids. The story of this exploit is now legendary. In the winter of 1901, Abd al-Aziz set out from Kuwait with a hand-picked band of forty

Figure 13. King Abd al-Aziz ("Ibn Saud"). Photo by Saudi Aramco.

men, heading south and east into the desert. After spending some time in al-Hasa, he came up to Riyadh from the south in mid-January 1902. Splitting his force (which had grown to about sixty men), he proceeded toward the city walls, telling those left behind to make for Kuwait if they heard nothing from him in twenty-four hours. At the walls, he left twenty men under his brother, Muhammad, to await the signal of success or failure. With ten men, he stole over the wall and broke into a house across the street from the al-Mismak fort, where the Rashidi governor, Ajlan, spent the night as a security precaution. Abd al-Aziz and his men waited for dawn, drinking coffee and reading the Quran.

In the morning, as Ajlan left the fort for his home, the invaders rushed his small party. Abd al-Aziz's cousin, Abdallah ibn Jaluwi, threw a spear at Ajlan that missed and broke off in the fortress gate, where it remained for many years. Ajlan ran for the fort. After a brief struggle at the postern gate, he was dispatched by Abdallah ibn Jaluwi, who then gained entrance to the fort. The garrison quickly surrendered, and the Al Sauds again became masters of Riyadh.

Abd al-Rahman, who had already decided that his son was better able than he to restore Saudi political fortunes, abdicated his claim to secular rule over Najd. However, he retained the more religious title, imam, which he kept until his death in 1928. Thereafter, no Saudi ruler has used that title. For the remainder of his life, Abd al-Rahman remained a close confidant of his son, Abd al-Aziz, who consulted him constantly on matters of state and deferred to his senior rank on ceremonial occasions.

Following the recapture of Riyadh, Abd al-Aziz immediately set out to restore the allegiance of the Najdi tribes, relying on his personal charisma; political marriages (Muslims are allowed four wives concurrently); and the growing unpopularity of the brutal new Rashidi amir, Abd al-Aziz ibn Rashid, who had succeeded his uncle, Muhammad, a few years before. Nevertheless, it took some twenty years for Rashidi power to be broken totally. Its downfall was in some measure due to rivalries within the Al Rashid family itself. Abd al-Aziz ibn Rashid was killed by Saudi troops in 1906, but it was not until 1921 that Abd al-Aziz finally subdued the Al Rashids and captured their capital, Ha'il.

In order to defeat the Al Rashids, Abd al-Aziz realized that he needed more than the promise of plunder to keep the loyalty of traditionally fickle tribes. A firm believer in the Muwahhidin revival, he raised the banner of Tawhid as his forefathers had done; but unlike them, he created a whole class of fanatical, ascetic Islamic warriors—the *Ikhwan*, or "the Brethren"—whom he settled in agricultural settlements located in Najdi oases. By 1912, the Ikhwan settler-warriors numbered 11,000. The following year, they wrested al-Hasa back from Ottoman control.

In the outside world, the creation of the third Najdi state was as unheralded as its two predecessors. Hardly anyone noticed when, in 1912, Abd al-Aziz elevated Najd from an amirate to the Sultanate of Najd and Its Dependencies in recognition of its increased size and importance.

But as war clouds gathered in the years leading up to World War I, Arabia again came into world focus. The British were seeking to counter rising German influence in the eastern Arab provinces of the Ottoman Empire, and Abd al-Aziz was seeking to counter Ottoman support for the Al Rashids. In 1910, Captain W. H. I. Shakespear, the British political agent in Kuwait, informally contacted Abd al-Aziz and, in 1913, visited him in Riyadh while on a trek through Arabia.

British interest in central Arabia quickened on the eve of the war. In 1914, Shakespear was sent to Riyadh as the British political representative to Abd al-Aziz and was with him the following January when Saudi forces attacked the Rashidi forces at Jarab. After initial success, the Saudis were pushed back and finally broke in disorder. Shakespear, dressed in a British uniform and directing the fire of a single artillery piece, was killed. In December 1915, Abd al-Aziz met personally at 'Uqayr on the Gulf coast with Sir Percy Cox, the new British political agent in Kuwait. There they concluded a treaty of friendship in which the British recognized Abd al-Aziz as the Sultan of Najd and al-Hasa and gave him a small stipend.

In the wake of Shakespear's death, central Arabia ceased to play a prominent role in British war plans. The British focused instead on the Hijaz in western Arabia. In 1915, Sir Henry McMahon, the British high commissioner in Cairo, promised Sharif Husayn of Makkah that the British would support Arab independence if he would rebel against Ottoman rule. In June 1916, Husayn proclaimed the Arab Revolt, assumed the title King of the Hijaz, and thereby became Britain's chosen instrument in Arabia. It was from the Hijaz that Colonel T. E. Lawrence (Lawrence of Arabia) launched his attacks against the Turks along the Hijaz railroad running south from Damascus to al-Madinah.

Because both the Hijaz and Najd were allied with the British against the Ottomans during the war, Abd al-Aziz had refrained from hostilities against Sharif Husayn. Following the war, however, hostilities became virtually inevitable. Husayn was an ambitious man and, in leading the Arab Revolt, may have aspired to replace the Ottoman sultan as caliph of Islam. To Husayn, Abd al-Aziz was probably no more than another desert chieftain and a proponent of a dangerous and fanatical, if not heretical, religious revival movement in the bargain.

To Abd al-Aziz, a proud desert aristocrat and a devout adherent of the Muwahhidin revival, the worldly Husayn was hard to accept as custodian of the two holiest sites in Islam, Makkah and al-Madinah. Moreover, in 1912, Husayn captured Abd al-Aziz's brother, S'ad, and released him only when Abd al-Aziz agreed to humiliating terms. Bad feeling also existed among the two leaders' sons. In 1919, Sharif Husayn's son Faysal snubbed Abd al-Aziz's son Faysal when they met in Paris as the Versailles Conference was in progress.

The first armed clash between the Saudis and the Hashimites occurred in May 1918. The Najdi 'Utayba tribal region on the frontier of the Hijaz was the source of friction. Husayn sent his son Abdallah (later king of Jordan) with an army to capture the 'Utayba town of Khurma. The Sharifian army was camped at nearby Turaba when the Ikhwan attacked and virtually annihilated it. An old 'Utayba tribesman who had been at the battle told me fifty years later that only those with horses (about one hundred, including Abdallah) escaped. "Thank God I had a horse," he added, indicating for the first time which side he had been on.

Abd al-Aziz still did not press his advantage, but the Ikhwan were getting more and more belligerent. Under Faysal al-Dawish, paramount shaykh of the Mutayr, they defeated Kuwaiti forces twice in 1920 and began raiding farther north. In 1921, after years of intermittent fighting, they finally occupied the Rashidi capital of Ha'il. To make peace with the Shammar tribes, Abd al-Aziz married the widow of Amir Saud ibn Rashid, who had been murdered by a cousin a year before, and adopted his children.

To prevent further border hostilities, Najd, Kuwait, and Iraq defined their common borders in 1922 in the 'Uqayr Protocol, creating the Kuwaiti and Iraqi neutral zones. Far more than Iraq and Kuwait, however, the Ikhwan coveted the Hijaz and the holy cities of Makkah and al-Madinah. Moreover, Abd al-Aziz felt that he was being surrounded by hostile Hashimite regimes. Following World War I, Husayn had proclaimed himself King of the Arabs. The British had made one of his sons, Faysal, king of Iraq and another son, Abdallah, amir of Transjordan, both newly created countries with the status of British mandates. Amir Abdallah's growing relations with the Al Rashids was one reason why Abd al-Aziz finally annexed the Rashidi amirate in 1921. He had hesitated before then because of the political upheavals of World War I.

Even after the war he was loath to confront Husayn directly, who was still an ally of the British. The final straw occurred in 1924. On March 3, Turkey abolished the caliphate; and two days later, Sharif (now King) Husayn proclaimed himself Caliph of all Muslims. That was more than the Ikhwan could take, and Abd al-Aziz invaded the Hijaz. In August, the Ikhwan took Ta'if without resistance; but when a shot rang out, the ensuing melee resulted in a massacre of the inhabitants. The terrified Hijazis pressured Husayn to abdicate. His son and successor, Ali, whose control was by then limited to Jiddah, fared no better. In December 1925, he surrendered to the Saudis and followed his father into exile. In January 1926, Abd al-Aziz was proclaimed "King of the Hijaz and Sultan of Najd and Its Dependencies."

After several years of negotiating border agreements with British protectorate and mandate states, Abd al-Aziz finally gained international recognition in the Treaty of Jiddah, negotiated with Sir Gilbert Clayton and signed in 1927. The British recognized the new Saudi state, the name of which was changed to the Kingdom of the Hijaz and Najd and Its Dependencies. Although the new name implied a unitary state, Najd and the Hijaz continued to be ruled separately for a number of years—the latter administered by the king's second surviving son, Prince Faysal, who was appointed viceroy.

In 1930, Abd al-Aziz annexed 'Asir south of the Hijaz, which his son Faysal had taken in 1924. Yemen continued to contest Saudi sovereignty over Wadi Najran, on the Yemen-'Asir frontier, until 1934 when it lost a brief war with the Saudis. The Saudi troops were commanded by Faysal and his older brother, Prince Saud, the heir apparent. Abd al-Aziz asked for no further territorial concessions, but the resulting Treaty of Ta'if laid to rest the border dispute until it was revived again in the 1980s. Thus, by 1930 Saudi territories were fairly well defined, with the exception of undemarcated borders and a few remaining border disputes. The most important outstanding land border dispute was over the Buraymi oasis on the Saudi/Abu Dhabi/Omani frontier. Although the Saudis had not controlled it since Imam Faysal's day, they had not relinquished their claim. Saudi-British arbitration in the 1950s failed to settle the problem, but in April 1974 the Saudis finally gave up their claim in return for various territorial and other concessions.

On September 22, 1932, the name of the country was officially changed to the Kingdom of Saudi Arabia. Thus, in a space of thirty years, Abd al-Aziz, starting out from exile with a band of forty men, had restored the Saudi patrimony. Although he did not know it at the time, he had also set the stage for the creation of the world's greatest oil power.

Even before the kingdom was fully consolidated in 1932, Abd al-Aziz realized that he would have to temper the militant zeal of the Ikhwan.[7] Following the annexation of the Hijaz and ʿAsir and the demarcation of borders with Transjordan and Iraq, there were few battlefields left to contest. The Ikhwan became restless with inactivity and were even more discontented with the introduction of modern technology such as autos, airplanes, and telephones, which they considered the devil's devices.

Conditions began to get out of hand in 1928 when Faysal al-Dawish, paramount shaykh of the Mutayr, and other tribal leaders raised the banner of revolt and began raiding in neighboring Iraq and Kuwait, bringing British retaliation with airplanes and motorized infantry. A face-off with the king was inevitable and came in 1929, when warriors loyal to the king wiped out the rebels at the battle of al-Sibila, probably the last great Bedouin battle in history. The independent military power of the tribes was broken forever.

The Ikhwan was more or less disbanded, although tribal levies were again used in 1934 during the brief war with Yemen. In 1956, tribal warriors were again organized into a paramilitary fighting force that became the nucleus of the present-day national guard.

From Desert Kingdom to Modern Oil State

When Abd al-Aziz annexed the Hijaz in 1926, it had a more sophisticated government than Najd, which was ruled on a highly informal and personalized basis. The Hijaz had a Consultative Council (*Majlis al-Shura*) and a Council of Ministers (*Majlis al-Wuzara'*). The king left much of the Hijazi governmental machinery in place, and for many years it was used in public administration for the entire country. Major decisions, however, were made wherever the king was, mainly in Riyadh.

The first two national ministries were the Ministry of Foreign Affairs and the Ministry of Finance (later Finance and National Economy). The former was established in 1930 and headed by Faysal, who was also viceroy of the Hijaz. Faysal was to retain the position of foreign minister (with one short interlude) until his death in 1975. The Finance Ministry was created in 1932 and for a time undertook whatever other government tasks the king wanted until separate ministries were created.[8] From this modest beginning, modern governmental institutions were gradually introduced until, shortly before King Abd al-Aziz's death in 1953, the government had so increased in size and complexity that the king established the Council of Ministers.

In the 1930s, the greatest obstacle to development was poverty. The kingdom was so poor that the finance minister, Abdallah Sulayman, kept the government accounts in a large black ledger, which, legend has it, he kept at home under his bed. Not only was Saudi Arabia one of the poorest countries on earth, but its economic situation was deteriorating as a result of the world depression and growing tensions leading to World War II. The major source of government revenue was receipts from the annual Hajj; and with the combination of worsening international economic and political conditions, Hajj receipts had declined greatly. Oil was discovered in commercial quantities in 1938, but the kingdom was not able to exploit it because of the advent of the war.

It was not until after World War II that oil revenues began to be a factor in the economic and political history of the kingdom. During the war, the United States agreed to a lend-lease agreement with Abd al-Aziz to keep the country solvent when the oil companies, which had been advancing him monies based on future earnings, were no longer financially able to do so.

The history of Saudi Arabia since the war has been one of unprecedented social and economic development, funded almost entirely by oil revenues. So fast did the pace of development proceed that impressive projects of one decade were torn down and replaced by even more impressive projects in the next. By the time King Abd al-Aziz died in 1953, he had created a firm foundation for building the modern oil state that is Saudi Arabia today. It is doubtful that he fully understood the implications of the steps he was taking, but neither did the outside world. Becoming accustomed to the steady flow of relatively cheap Saudi oil, the world soon took the country for granted and turned its attention to other, more pressing matters.

Abd al-Aziz was succeeded by his eldest surviving son, Saud. (His eldest son, Turki, died in the influenza pandemic of 1919.) A well-meaning person and an able politician in the traditional desert mold, Saud was unable to cope with the growing complexities that oil wealth and rapid modernization created. His reign was characterized by palace intrigue, large-scale corruption, and waste. Despite unprecedented oil revenues, the kingdom was virtually bankrupt.

In 1958, King Saud was pressured into naming as prime minister his half-brother Faysal ibn Abd al-Aziz. Faysal, who was the heir apparent and had been foreign minister since 1930, took over the reins of government and began both fiscal and administrative reforms. In 1960 Saud again took over the government, and Faysal retired to private life. It became increasingly apparent, however, that Saud's mismanagement was threatening the viability of the kingdom. By October 1962, Faysal was being urged by many Al Saud members and religious leaders (the ʿulama) to accept the kingship; but he declined, citing his promise to his father to support his half-brother Saud.

In 1962, Faysal became prime minister for the second time, with his half-brother Khalid as deputy prime minister. In many ways, 1962 was the beginning of a continuity of government that has lasted to the present day. Faysal appointed two half-brothers, Fahd (now king) and Sultan, as ministers of the interior and of defense and aviation respectively, and a third, Abdallah, as commander of the national guard. Among the more prominent and able technocrats appointed in 1962 was Ahmad Zaki Yamani, who as minister of petroleum and mineral resources played a major role in the kingdom's coming of age as a major oil power.

King Saud's pride made it difficult for him to accept the role of ceremonial monarch, and he repeatedly challenged Faysal in order to regain full governing powers. Finally, in late October 1964, the Al Sauds, supported by leading religious leaders and others, forced Saud to abdicate. The religious leadership issued a *fatwa* (a binding Islamic legal opinion) proclaiming Faysal king. Saud held on to power briefly, but on November 3, 1964, he abdicated and left Riyadh for the last time. A sick and broken man, he died in Greece in 1969.

If King Abd al-Aziz was the creator of the modern Saudi state, King Faysal was the architect of the modern oil kingdom.[9] The current trends in Saudi economic and social development and domestic and foreign policies all began during his reign. Faysal was killed in 1975 by a deranged nephew, Khalid ibn Musaʿid. At the time of his death, he was easily the senior statesman of the entire Arab world and a recognized world leader as well.

King Faysal's experience in foreign affairs began with an official visit to England in 1919 when he was seventeen years old. On his way home, he visited the Versailles peace conference. He was also, with a two-year hiatus, Saudi Arabia's foreign minister from the creation of the ministry until his death; and as foreign minister, he attended the San Francisco conference creating the United Nations. As king, he attended Arab summits and made official visits to the major capitals of the world. With this background, he was always comfortable in dealings with his Arab neighbors and the world at large.

King Faysal also was formidable in his grasp of Islamic law, the constitutional basis of the regime. His mother was an Al al-Shaykh, and from her

Figure 14. King Faysal ibn Abd al-Aziz Al Saud. Photo by Information Office, Royal Embassy of Saudi Arabia.

family he became so well versed in Islam that ultraconservative figures who attempted to oppose his modernization policies on religious grounds found that he was equally or more knowledgeable of the holy law than they were.

Perhaps the most notable aspect of King Faysal's reign was his ability to gauge just how far and how fast he could nudge his people toward modernity without exceeding a pace they could assimilate. He was also committed to preserving an Islamic society in Saudi Arabia and maintaining an Islamic political system. This careful approach often frustrated Westerners who wished to see Saudi Arabia transformed overnight into a representative democracy.

In 1962, largely in response to urging by President Kennedy, Faysal issued a ten-point political reform plan. Committed to maintaining the Islamic political system espoused by the Muwahhidin revival, however, the king was in no rush to import alien Western political institutions. The U.S. government, seeing little progress on implementation of the reform plan, instructed successive American ambassadors from time to time to raise the issue of political reform with him. I recall one such demarche made in the late 1960s when American antiwar riots were rampant. The king replied by asking the ambassador whether the United States really wanted the kingdom to be turned into another Berkeley campus.[10]

King Faysal was succeeded by his half-brother, Khalid bin Abd al-Aziz. The new king was a pious, introspective person who lacked his predecessor's flair for government. Preferring to keep a low profile, he delegated much of the day-to-day running of the government to his half-brother, Prince Fahd, the new heir apparent. There was virtually no change in government policies and programs, and most of the veteran cabinet members appointed by Faysal remained in office.

Because of the high visibility of Prince Fahd and other members of the government—both royal family and technocrats—Khalid's role as king has been somewhat underestimated by outsiders. Despite his retiring ways, he was still very much in charge and had a talent for arbitrating among rival princes and technocrats and maintaining a consensus on the direction the kingdom ought to take. He was also popular among the people, who respected him for his modesty and piety.

Khalid, never in good health, died of a heart attack in June 1982. He was succeeded by Fahd in a smooth transition. Prince Abdallah, the head of the national guard, was named first deputy prime minister and heir apparent. Fahd's full brother, Prince Sultan, was named second deputy prime minister and second in line of succession.

Fahd brought to the office of king a great deal of experience. He was appointed education minister in 1953 and interior minister in 1962, an office he held until he became heir apparent in 1975. Like Khalid before him, Fahd maintained the kingdom on the same basic course established by King Faysal and with much of the same leadership. In the intervening years, however, new faces began to appear as older ones stepped down. A notable change was the replacement of Ahmad Zaki Yamani with Hisham Nazir as petroleum minister. Yamani, always considered "Faysal's man" since he was appointed petroleum minister in 1962, retired to private life after a long and distinguished career. In the summer of 1995, Fahd again reshuffled the cabinet and retired many senior bureaucrats, a move apparently motivated by his desire to infuse the government with new blood. The most noted ministers to step down were the finance minister, Muhammad Aba al-Khayl, and the petroleum minister, Hisham Nazir, both of whom had long, distinguished careers in public service.

The task of maintaining economic and social development while resisting secularization, difficult in Faysal's time, has become even more difficult in succeeding years. Most Saudis have been satisfied with the direction that Saudi development is taking. On the fringes, however, are those who wish to see more rapid evolution to the type of society and political systems found in the West and, in direct contradistinction, those who fear that modernization has

Figure 15. King Fahd ibn Abd al-Aziz Al Saud. Photo by Saudi Aramco.

brought too much secularization and wish to return to a more strict social and political order based on the Wahhabi revival. In trying to steer between the two extremes, King Fahd expanded social and economic programs but also took care to link state policies closely to Islamic precepts. In October 1986, he assumed the title *Khadim al-Haramayn*, or "Custodian of the Two Holy Places" (that is, Makkah and al-Madinah), a reflection of the Islamic nature of the regime.

In the history of Saudi Arabia, one sees an often turbulent and sometimes retrogressive but nevertheless steady development from a desert principality to a modern oil state. In the future, however, the challenges will be even greater. Among the most important will be dealing with the increasingly complex problems of a rapidly developing, modern, affluent oil state juxtaposed with a conservative, traditional Islamic society—and doing so while broadening the base of public participation in the political process.

Among other major changes has been the explosion in education. When Prince Faysal appointed his cabinet in 1962, there were scarcely a dozen men in the entire kingdom with a college degree. Today there are more people in cabinet and subcabinet positions holding doctorates than there are in the United States.

The full effects of social change brought on by rapid social and economic development programs will probably not be fully realized for years to come. Changing attitudes have produced a generation gap. For example, whereas the current leadership, including the king, spent their formative years in near poverty, the younger generation has never really experienced economic hardship.

Thus, the level of expectations as the result of oil wealth and education will probably continue to increase as younger people rise to positions of leadership and influence or, conversely, are denied access into the bureaucracy because of overstaffing and rapid population growth.

Change is also likely to beget more change. Government operations, a personalized and somewhat haphazard endeavor under King Abd al-Aziz, have become much more institutionalized in the years since his death. Recently, more focus has been placed on a growing desire among the public, particularly younger people, for participation in the political process. In early 1992, after a decade of deliberations, King Fahd announced the creation of the *Majlis al-Shura* (Consultative Council). It is not an elective body, but it is intended as a step toward broadening public participation. The future history of Saudi Arabia will center on how the society reacts to change and the regime's ability to accommodate that change.

3

The Saudi Political System

Saudi Arabia is a harsh land, and until the discovery of oil, mere physical survival was a struggle. The imperative of survival bred harsh rules of behavior and swift punishment for nonconformity, which are still tightly woven into the social and political fabric of the country. One of the characteristics—indeed, anomalies—of Saudi politics is a harsh political system administered with a relatively light touch.

The Saudi Constitutional System

Saudi Arabia has always been ruled under Islamic law. The most recently reaffirmation of that fact is stated in article 1 of the Basic Law of Government, issued by King Fahd in a royal decree on March 1, 1992: "The Saudi Arabian Kingdom is a sovereign Arab Islamic state with Islam as its religion; God's book [the Quran] and the Sunna [the Traditions, or inspired sayings of the prophet Muhammad] are its constitution; Arabic is its language; and Riyadh is its capital."[1]

Unlike Christianity, which is largely a theological system, Islam is primarily a legal system based on divine law. Islamic dogma is quite simple, consisting of five basic pillars (tenets) of the faith. The first, profession of faith, is the most important and is really all that is required of a believer. It is expressed in the *Shahada:* "La allah ila Allah wa Muhammad Rasul Allah" [There is no god but God, and Muhammad is the messenger of God]. The other pillars are prayer (five times a day, facing Makkah), alms, fasting during the Muslim lunar month of Ramadan, and making the Hajj to Makkah once during a lifetime if one is physically and financially able.

Another tenet, sometimes called the "sixth pillar," is *jihad.* Often translated as "holy war," it is actually a much broader concept, referring to both the private and corporate obligation to encourage virtue and resist evil—albeit by force, if necessary. Modern Islamic puritanical revolutionaries, in calling for jihad, obviously emphasize the use of force. In Saudi Arabia, a nonmilitary manifestation of this obligation is the *mutawaʿin*; often called the religious police, their official designation is the Committee for Propagating Virtue and Suppressing Evil.

Islamic law, or *Shariʿa* (literally, "the pathway"), is much more complex than Islamic theology and is the primary area of specialization by Islamic scholars. Despite theological differences among the various sects of Islam (for example, between Sunnis and Shiʿas), Islamic law is universally respected by all Muslims. The sources of the law are the Quran and the Sunna, the latter comprised of *Hadiths*—specific divinely inspired sayings of the prophet. (Shiʿas also consider sayings of Ali and other Shiʿa imams as divinely inspired.)

The Saudi legal system is based on Sunni interpretations of Islamic law, principally but not exclusively according to the Hanbali school of Islamic jurisprudence.[2] Hanbali law is the most conservative of all the Sunni schools, particularly in family law. Thus, many of the conservative social practices observed in Saudi Arabia, such as veiling of women in public, while not specifically required by Shariʿa law, certainly have the backing of the religious establishment.

On the other hand, Hanbali law is among the most liberal of the schools on commercial practices. It is no coincidence that commercial practices in the kingdom are much more free-wheeling than many Westerners are used to. It would be a mistake, however, to assume that anything goes in doing business in Saudi Arabia.

Islamic law is supreme in Saudi Arabia, even over the king, who may be taken to court. A special tribunal called the *Diwan al-Mazalim* (Board of Grievances) has been created to hear cases against the government. Thus, despite no formal separation of powers and without democratically elected representatives, Saudi Arabia is not an absolute monarchy in the historic European sense. The doctrine of "the divine right of kings" would be considered heresy.

All modern states must have some contemporary regulatory codes; and the Shariʿa, developed 1,200 to 1,400 years ago, obviously does not directly address the legal issues of a modern, technological world. Nevertheless, there is a means for dealing with issues not mentioned in Islamic law. Unlike Western law, in which acts are either legal or illegal, the Shariʿa includes five categories—*wajib*, acts that are obligatory; *mandub*, in which commission is recommended and will bring reward but omission will not bring punishment; *makruh*, where omission brings reward but commission does not bring punishment; *haram*, acts that are prohibited; and *mubah*, acts that are not specifically addressed in the Holy Law, and about which it is indifferent.[3] This fifth category, mubah, has been used as a legal loophole by many Islamic countries for inserting entire Western legal codes into their legal systems. Conversely, many present-day Islamic fundamentalist reformers seek to reestablish the frontiers of the Shari'a by shrinking the scope of secular legal norms under this category and subordinating them to Islamic legal norms.

The Saudi experience is different. The government never embraced Western secular legal norms. Indeed, in 1927, when Abd al-Aziz was still consolidating what was to become the Kingdom of Saudi Arabia, the 'ulama of Najd ('ulama are Islamic religious authorities; the singular is 'alim) issued a fatwa (a binding legal opinion) denying him the right to make statutory law.[4]

In place of statutory legislation, royal decrees (*nizams*) have been promulgated over the years. Their relationship to Shari'a law is somewhat analogous to the relationship in the United States between implementing regulations created by government agencies and statutory legislation. Thus, although there is no comprehensive Saudi criminal, civil, or commercial code, the nizams provide a basis for regulating secular and commercial transactions in conformity with the Shari'a. In addition, special administrative tribunals have been created to adjudicate labor and commercial disputes.

SAUDI POLITICAL DYNAMICS

Before discussing Saudi political institutions and the political process, let us turn first to the dynamics of Saudi politics. Three areas are particularly important: political culture, political ideology, and the decision-making process.

Saudi Political Culture

Saudi political culture here refers to the impact of traditional Islamic cultural norms on Saudi political behavior. In a seminal article on the influence of traditional Islamic culture on politics, James Bill writes, "The traditional Islamic system has possessed remarkable resiliency and resistance to transformation. As a result, contemporary Islamic societies are the scene of particularly intense conflict between the forces of tradition and modernity. A deeper understanding of this struggle requires an examination of the forces and characteristics that infused these traditional systems with extraordinary elasticity."[5]

Saudi culture is overwhelmingly Islamic and traditional. Islam is more than a religion; it is a totally self-contained, cosmic system. The emphasis here is on cultural values, not religious piety. These norms have been particularly resilient in the face of change despite the mammoth pace of modernization in the country.

One behavioral characteristic clearly linked to the kingdom's traditional Islamic culture is a pronounced sense of the inevitability of events. Based on the Islamic emphasis on the omnipotence of God's will, it is often expressed in the Arabic phrase *Insha'allah*, or "God willing." If God does not will something, it cannot possibly happen, including events in a person's life that might normally be considered within the realm of personal responsibility. To outsiders, Saudis sometimes appear to use this Islamic concept of God's will as an excuse to abdicate personal responsibility—for example, in meeting some obligation. It would be a mistake, however, to call into question the subordination of personal will to the will of God.

This characteristic has often been called "Islamic fatalism" and as such can denote passivity. Total faith in God's will can be quite the opposite, however, as evidenced by the fanaticism of Islamist extremist groups throughout the region, which are convinced they are instruments of God's will. Faith in the inevitability of God's will can also enable decision makers to wait far longer than others might for a desired outcome. Patience is a watchword of Saudi politics.

Two other traditional Saudi cultural traits are associated with non-Western cultures generally, not just Islamic cultures: compartmentalization of behavior and personalization of behavior. Compartmentalization (or atomization) of behavior is a tendency to view events from one single context at a time, not seeking to explore all the ramifications of how it might appear in other contexts. In an Islamic culture, it is reinforced by the concept that all causality is based on God's will. This reduces the necessity for different responses to a situation to appear consistent in different contexts. Although Saudi (and other Third World) decision makers are obviously no more prone to inconsistencies than anyone else, they do have a tendency not to focus on the possible impact of policy decisions on ancillary issues—for example, the economic impact of a political decision. It is common, therefore, for a single issue to elicit different and sometimes incompatible policy responses depending on the context or contexts in which it is viewed—such as national security interests, political interests, economic interests, and so on.

Because nearly all major policy issues are viewed from multiple contexts, it would be a mistake always to seek an overarching rationale in Saudi decision making. Saudi politics operate on many levels—Islamic world politics, Arab world politics, Saudi state politics, Saudi regional interests (Najdis from central Arabia tend to dominate the political system), tribal and extended family loyalties and obligations, and considerations of personal ambition. Probably the strongest loyalty is to the extended family; and among the Al Saud, no major Saudi political decision is ever totally devoid of considerations about how it will affect the family's welfare and survivability.

Saudi political behavior is also highly personalized. Personal rapport is the sine qua non of good political relations throughout the Middle East. Proximity to power begets power, and losing face is to be avoided at all costs.[6] As a result, an elaborate system guiding interpersonal relations has evolved. For example, a Saudi response to a question will almost always be calculated more for its effect on the other party than an indication of true feelings.

Personalization does not always equate with personal contact. In negotiating on substantive issues, most Saudis prefer to let others work out the details, enabling the principals to confirm agreements already reached and ensuring that neither party loses face if negotiations fail. A senior Saudi official once told me that it is not uncommon for a Saudi being considered for a high position to be approached first by his driver to find out whether or not he would be interested. If he says no, the matter will never be raised again (although if he says yes, he still might not get it).

Another manifestation of this characteristic is a tendency among Saudis to avoid giving a direct no to a proposal, but neither will they agree when they do not believe it is in their best interests to do so. In some cases, negotiations have dragged on for years over issues the Saudis have no intention of acceding to but will not directly say so.

A major implication of the personalization of behavior on Saudi politics is the influence of personal relationships on decision making. It is not enough to know the bureaucratic chain of command in seeking to understand how decisions are made. One must also know who can exert personal influence and on what range of decisions.

One other cultural characteristic not directly associated with Islam is the high degree of Saudi ethnocentricity, due mainly to the country's historical isolation and geographical insularity. Arabia is the cradle of both Arabs and Islam, and Saudis tend to see themselves as the center of their universe. Personal status is conferred more by bloodlines than money or achievement, and nearly all Saudis claim a proud Arabian ancestry. Having never been under Western colonial rule, Saudis have never developed a national inferiority complex or other psychological baggage acquired by many colonialized peoples. They see themselves not merely as equals of the West but in fact believe their Islamic cultural values to be vastly superior to Western secular values. Close personal relationships aside, they tend to look on outsiders in aggregate as people to be tolerated only as long as they have something to contribute.

Saudi Political Ideology

For the past 250 years, the teachings of Muhammad ibn Abd al-Wahhab have constituted the political ideology of Saudi Arabia. His revival movement has provided the Saudi regime with an egalitarian, universal, and moral ideology that has served to bind rulers and ruled together through many crises and troubles. Indeed, one could argue that Abd al-Wahhab's Islamic revival is the ideological glue that has allowed the Saudi state to survive the 250 years of its often turbulent history.

One must use care, however, not to look at the revival as a political ideology independent of Islam. It is based on the Hanbali school of Sunni Islamic jurisprudence and the teachings of the early Hanbali political theorist, Taqi al-Din Ahmad Ibn Taymiyya (died 1328).[7] Ibn Taymiyya lived at a time when the Abbasid caliphate of Baghdad was in decline, and many petty Muslim rulers were seeking fatwas from local religious authorities—often through bribes—declaring their legitimacy as independent rulers. He denounced this practice and claimed that political legitimacy came only from strict adherence to the fundamental teachings of Shari'a law. It is not surprising, therefore, that Ibn Taymiyya spent most of his adult life in jail.

Ibn Taymiyya's call for a return to the fundamentals of Islam and the rejection of false innovations that had crept into the religion appealed to Muhammad ibn Abd al-Wahhab. Ibn Taymiyya was not just another puritan fundamentalist, however. Beginning in the ninth century, most Sunni Islamic jurists ceased to recognize independent reasoning (*ijtihad*) as an authoritative means of interpreting Islamic law. Ibn Taymiyya not only rejected what was called the "closing of the door of independent reasoning" but claimed to be a *mujtahid* (a qualified practitioner).

One of his most creative reinterpretations was that of the concept of *jahiliyya*, "the age of ignorance," which in Islamic historiography refers to the period before Islam. Ibn Taymiyya claimed that the term applied not only to those who lived before Islam but to people still living who did not follow God's law. Moreover, it was the obligation of the entire Muslim community to rise up in jihad against such people—using force, if necessary. The injunction to fight not only enemies of Islam but also heretics within Islam makes Ibn Taymiyya's teachings potentially one of the most revolutionary political ideologies in Islamic history. This concept forms the ideological backbone of many of the militant Islamic fundamentalist revolutionary and terrorist groups today. For such groups, acts of political violence are raised to a moral imperative, jihad.

The Saudi regime itself was initially quite militant, waging war against its neighbors not only to pursue bounty and empire, but also to propagate good and oppose evil. Over the years, it has lost some of its revolutionary fervor but not its puritan, fundamentalist principles. It is conceivable, therefore, that under the right conditions—such as the growing frustrations and perceived injustices of an ever-stressful world—the teachings of Muhammad ibn Abd al-Wahhab and Ibn Taymiyya could once again become the rallying cry of those seeking revolutionary change.

The Saudi Decision-Making Process

The Saudi political decision-making process often appears arbitrary and capricious to the casual observer, but it does contain a systemic logic. The creation of formal institutions over the past sixty years has made government operations a great deal more orderly but has not fundamentally changed the informal process at the heart of the system.

This informal process incorporates two fundamental concepts: *ijma* "(consensus) and *shura* (consultation). Consensus has been used to legitimize decisions in the Arab world for millennia and has even been incorporated into Islam. The consensus of the entire Muslim community on a matter of interpretation of the Shari'a is considered authoritative. Even a Saudi king, despite all the powers concentrated in him, cannot act without consensus. With a consensus, the government can move with astonishing speed; without it, years can go by with no decision made. Thus, one of the chief tasks of the king (and, by extension, all subordinate Saudi decision makers) is to create a consensus for action and then to implement it. The king is both chief consensus maker and chief executive.

In order to create a consensus of support, a leader must engage in consultation (shura) with those deemed most competent, influential, and personally loyal to him. Shura is a two-way street, with the person consulted actively participating in the decision-making process. Arabic has another word for consultation, *tashawir*, which means merely soliciting an opinion. This type of consultation also takes place in Saudi Arabia, but it does not constitute participation in the political process.

In the oil age, the consultation/consensus decision-making system is under heavy pressure. Government operations are too large and complicated for this traditional, personalized process always to work effectively or fairly; and as a result, decisions are becoming more capricious. Even when a leader seeks to engage in shura, he can end up with tashawir, rationalizing that the people who were consulted were participating in the process. Still, for any sustained increase in public participation in the decision-making process, it will probably be necessary for the process to incorporate some form of the consultation-consensus process.

SAUDI POLITICAL INSTITUTIONS

Other than the formal Islamic legal system administered by the religious establishment and the informal, unwritten tribal law governing the behavior of tribal leaders, Saudi rulers had almost no formal political institutions until the capture of the Hijaz in 1925. Najd was ruled by Abd al-Aziz in a highly personalized way through shura with leading members of the royal family, tribal and religious leaders, and an entourage of confidants, all of whom were members of the royal *diwan* (court). It is interesting to note that one of his most trusted confidants was his sister, Nura. The Hijaz, on the other hand, had a much more formal system of government, including cabinet ministers.

When Abd al-Aziz captured the Hijaz, he left its political institutions intact. He realized the need to reassure the local inhabitants and the Muslim world in general that rule of law in the Muslim holy places would prevail and that the safety of the persons and properties of all pilgrims would be protected. The Hijaz with its holy cities of Makkah and al-Madinah was important to Abd al-Aziz not only for spiritual reasons, but for economic reasons as well. Before the discovery of oil, Hajj receipts constituted the primary foreign-exchange earner, propping up the entire economy.

The early development of Saudi national political institutions, therefore, can be seen as a process by which more advanced Hijazi institutions were slowly, and with little planning, adapted to the political and bureaucratic needs of the country as a whole. Paralleling this development was the evolution of public policy making from a totally personalized system run directly by the king to a more institutionalized system, still highly personalized but with a more bureaucratic structure and more standardized procedures.

On August 29, 1926, Abd al-Aziz promulgated a new Hijazi constitution, al-Taʿlimat al-Asasiyya lil-Mamlaka al-Hijaziyya (the Basic Instructions for the Kingdom of the Hijaz).[8] The Basic Instructions reaffirmed many of the political institutions already in existence in the Hijaz. Public administration was divided into six basic areas—foreign affairs, finance, internal affairs (interior), education, Shariʿa (judicial) affairs, and military affairs. In 1927 the first three were institutionalized into agencies, and in 1931 they were elevated to ministries. Most of the governmental machinery was handled by interior, which included departments of public health, public instruction, posts and telegraphs, maritime health and quarantine, public security, Islamic courts, and municipalities. Executive powers were vested in a viceroy, King Abd al-Aziz's second surviving son, Prince Faysal bin Abd al-Aziz.

Initially, there were some institutional holdovers from the Sharifian administration. For example, both Jiddah and Makkah continued to be administered by a town governor (qaymmaqam), and the major towns had municipal councils. On the other hand, provincial governors, or amirs, were appointed by and reported directly to the king, as was the case throughout the country. They chosen for the most part from members of the royal family, including collateral branches of the family such as the Bin Jaluwis, or from closely associated families such as the al-Sudayris.

The Basic Instructions also provided for the Consultative Council (Majlis al-Shura), whose members were appointed. Reorganized in 1928, it functioned as a quasi-legislative body presided over by the viceroy. Although it was never formally abolished, the Hijazi Majlis al-Shura fell into disuse and ceased to function by the mid-1930s.

The closest thing the Hijaz had to a formal cabinet was the Executive Council created in 1927 and chaired by the viceroy. It included ranking officials in foreign affairs and finance and the head of the Majlis al-Shura. In 1931, it was elevated to the Council of Deputies (*Majlis al-Nawab*); and while it technically had jurisdiction only in the Hijaz, its scope of activities increasingly expanded to include the whole kingdom. A less-structured viceregal diwan also was established and, like the royal diwan, also functioned somewhat like an inner cabinet. Many important princes and other leaders maintained regular diwans as a means of providing direct access to the leadership for the people.

Retaining a separate set of Hijazi political institutions did not mean that King Abd al-Aziz administered the Hijaz and Najd as totally separate entities. We have seen that the Council of Deputies served the entire country. The same held true for public administration, which was still highly personalized. Thus, if the king felt that a Hijazi ministry was the appropriate agency to perform some task in Najd or al-Hasa, it would be so tasked. Likewise, many of Prince Faysal's viceregal decrees were applied throughout the country as if they were royal decrees.

The first nationwide ministry to be created was the Ministry of Foreign Affairs, established in 1930 under Prince Faysal. Ambivalence existed even here because foreign affairs was an area covered in the Basic Instructions of the Hijaz and Prince Faysal, as viceroy, continued to be the Hijazi minister of foreign affairs as well. Of possibly more importance to the development of political institutions was the creation of the Ministry of Finance in 1932. Like foreign affairs, it initially overlapped with the separate Hijazi Finance Ministry, which continued to exist for a number of years. The new national Ministry of Finance was a far different institution than that of the present day, for during the 1930s and the first half of the 1940s Saudi Arabia was on the verge of bankruptcy. In 1954, the Finance Ministry merged with the Ministry of National Economy, created the previous year, to form the Ministry of Finance and National Economy.

The Finance Ministry was initially responsible for most of the administrative machinery of the entire kingdom, much as the Hijazi Ministry of Interior had previously been responsible for it. (The latter was abolished in June 1934.) Many of the subsequent national ministries thus began as departments under the Finance Ministry, some becoming independent agencies before being elevated to ministry level. In 1944 the Agency of Defense was raised to the Ministry of Defense (later Defense and Aviation), and in the 1950s several more ministries emerged—Interior, now concentrating only on public security (1951); Health (1951); Communications (1953); Agriculture and Water (1953); Education (1953); and Commerce and Industry (1954). In the 1960s the ministries of Petroleum and Mineral Resources (1960), Hajj and Awqaf ("religious endowments," singular *waqf*); Labor and Social Affairs (1962), and Information (1963) were created. In 1970 the Ministry of Justice was created and in 1975 the ministries of Posts, Telegraphs, and Telephones; Public Works; Municipal and Rural Affairs; Planning (formerly the Independent Central Planning Organization); Industry and Electricity; and Higher Education. In the summer of 1993, the Ministry of Hajj and Awqaf was divided into two separate ministries, increasing the number of Saudi ministries to twenty-one.

Local government has been a source of considerable confusion in Saudi Arabia. Most national ministries have officials in the regional provinces (called amirates) who report directly to the ministries in Riyadh, but they must also work closely under the regional amirs. The Regions Statute, issued by royal decree on March 1, 1992, does not greatly clarify the situation. Article 6 states that each regional amir must "supervise the organs of state and their employees in the region . . . , taking into account the ties of the employees of ministries and [agencies] with their competent authorities." Each amir must also have "direct contact" with the relevant national ministers and agency heads and keep the minister of interior informed. Although the interior minister is directly in charge of regional and local government, the decree confers the equal rank of minister on the regional amirs.[9]

There are currently sixteen regional amirates in Saudi Arabia, and the amirs include a number of the king's brothers. As of late 1995, they included Prince Salman in Riyadh, Prince Majid in Makkah (Western Province), Prince Abd al-Majid in al-Madinah, and Prince Muqrin in Qasim. Some of the next generation of princes were also regional amirs, including Prince Khalid Al Faysal in Asir and Prince Muhammad ibn Fahd (the king's son) in the Eastern Province. Prince Muhammad replaced Prince Abd al-Muhsin ibn Jaluwi, a member of the collateral Jaluwi branch of the Al Saud family that had made the Eastern Province virtually its own domain since the region was reconquered by Abd al-Aziz early in the century.

According to the decree, each amir will be responsible for subregional governates, districts, and local government centers. The decree also stipulated ten-man advisory councils for the regions, paralleling the nationwide Majlis al-Shura (discussed later in this chapter).

Special mention should be made of the Ministry of Justice, which forms the judicial branch of government. The head of the Islamic legal system traditionally held the title "grand mufti and chief qadi." A mufti is one who issues fatwas, and a qadi is the judge in an Islamic, or *quda*, court. To some degree, the creation of the Ministry of Justice was just a change in nomenclature, for many of the same people remained in roughly the same positions. But it was also an attempt to modernize the bureaucratic machinery of the Islamic legal system without changing the substance. The office of grand mufti and chief qadi had traditionally been given to a member of the Al al-Shaykh family, but King Faysal appointed as the first minister of justice a highly respected but forward-looking Islamic scholar, the late Shaykh Muhammad Harakan. Upon his retirement, transition to ministry status had been successfully made.

Unlike Western constitutional systems, the quda court system is located institutionally under the Ministry of Justice. This does not mean that it is subject to government whim. Basic to the whole idea of Islamic law is that it is above the government. Saudi judges are independent from government policy. But there is a major philosophical difference between the Saudi system of justice and those in the West. Rather than seek to determine the guilty party, the emphasis is on adjudication of disputes without loss of face, a reflection of the dynamics of a tribal society where disputes can go on for generations. The system is believed to be working best when the case is resolved before ever going to court.

The court system includes general courts and appeals courts. Because there is no case law in Saudi Arabia, judges are bound only to Islamic law, not to other rulings. The king acts as the final court of appeal and a source of pardon. King Abd al-Aziz was noted for dispensing justice of all kinds, but he refrained from challenging Islamic legal interpretations without first gaining the consensus of the 'ulama supporting his view. His successors have continued to exercise judicial powers but to an increasingly lesser extent as the judicial system has expanded over the years.

In 1993, the office of grand mufti was revived and conferred upon Shaykh Abd al-Aziz Ibn Baz, who was already head of the committee for fatwas. The reason behind the move was apparently to instill more bureaucratic discipline over the issuance of fatwas, but it is not certain what the relationship is between the grand mufti (a leading and very conservative Saudi religious scholar) and the minister of justice.

There are also administrative committees under the various ministries to adjudicate disputes. Westerners are most familiar with labor and commercial dispute settlement committees. In addition, there is the independent Diwan al-Mazalim (Board of Grievances), mentioned previously, that mainly hears cases between the government and private citizens.

It took more than fifty years after the promulgation of the Basic Instructions by King Abd al-Aziz for the current government structure of Saudi Arabia to emerge. One of Abd al-Aziz's last acts was to create the Council of Ministers (*Majlis al-Wuzara*'), which he decreed in October 1953, just a month before his death. Government operations continued to be highly personalized under his successors, but it was no longer the same degree of paternalistic, personal rule that had characterized the Saudi regime up to Abd al-Aziz. As oil wealth demanded a new type of leadership, more formal governmental institutions had to be put into place in order to make the transition possible.

The most recent major political institution to be created is the new Majlis al-shura (Consultative Council) decreed by King Fahd on March 1, 1992. In some respects, it completed the process of expanding Hijazi political institutions to the entire country. For years, there had been discussion of reviving the old Hijazi Majlis al-Shura, but no action had been taken. One of King Fahd's first stated priorities when he became king in 1982 was to create a new nationwide majlis, but it was ten more years before the idea was given substance. Some attributed the long delay to reluctance on the part of the regime. In fact, it was the 'ulama more than the regime that dragged their feet in determining what the new Majlis's responsibilities were to be. Harking back to the 1927 fatwa, many argued that any institution that created statutory law was contrary to the Shari 'a, which is considered a wholly self-contained system of revealed law.

A number of Western observers have also assessed the Saudi Majlis al-Shura as an embryonic parliament in the Western sense and a possible precursor to democratic representative government. Whether or not such a democratic institution will ever evolve in the kingdom, it is certainly not the concept on which the Majlis was modeled. King Fahd undoubtedly saw the need to expand public participation in the political process, but he has publicly rejected a Western-style democratic legislative body. Rather, he drew on the formal Islamic concept of shura to institutionalize what had been the informal means of political participation all along—consulting "people of knowledge and expertise and specialists" to come up with a consensus to legitimize public policy. With rapid modernization funded by oil revenues, it was increasingly obvious that the informal system was no longer adequate to create a true consensus. In the end, agreement was reached that the Majlis would be made up of sixty members and that it would suggest new decrees (regulatory law) and review and evaluate foreign and domestic policies.[10]

Although the first Council president, Muhammad ibn Ibrahim ibn Jubayr, was named in 1992 (he was formerly the minister of justice), it was more than a year later, in August 1993, before King Fahd appointed the first members. Council members are to serve four years and meet in closed session at least once every two weeks. Every member has the right to express his views on any subject referred to one of the Majlis's committees. The agenda will be determined by the Majlis president, deputy president, and committee chairmen.

Among the first appointees were businessmen, technocrats, diplomats, journalists, Islamic scholars, and professional soldiers, representing all regions of the country. Breaking with tradition, most were young by Saudi standards—in their forties and fifties. Thus, although most of them came from well-known families, they tended not to be the family patriarchs that speculation had suggested might be appointed. Many had doctorates from the United States, Europe, and the Middle East. Similarly, the Islamic scholars were young men with outside exposure, not the older generation of leaders of the 'ulama. One member was appointed from the Al al-Shaykh family, but he was a retired general.

In addition to creating the Majlis, King Fahd also issued decrees expanding the consultative role of the Council of Ministers.[11] Heretofore, the Council of Ministers, headed by the king as prime minister, seldom acted as a body. Its members ran their ministries almost independently of the others. Under the new decrees, the council will collectively approve loan contracts (backed by royal decree) as well as the national budget, international treaties, and concessions. To reduce conflict of interest, ministers can hold no other public or private positions and are forbidden to buy, sell, or loan government property. They (and other senior officials) can also serve no more than four years unless extended by the king. Invoking this provision in August 1995, King Fahd named fifteen new ministers and reshuffled three others after replacing 100 of 250 senior officials the previous month. The moves were generally interpreted as a means of acquiring and promoting deserving younger men.

Theoretically, the term limitations on the ministers will usher in a completely new Council of Ministers in two years. Given Saudi practice, however, that does not appear likely. Rather, the term limitations appear designed to provide a means to retire incumbents who are no longer effective. A more interesting question is whether the Council of Ministers will begin to act collegially as a single body. If so, it could conceivably evolve into an "upper house" in contrast to the Majlis al-Shura as a "lower house."

In sum, the main impact of the Consultative Council and the new mandate for the Council of Ministers is likely to be a formal institutionalization of a very old process—consultation—rather than the introduction of a new process of democratization. At the same time, the Islamic concept of shura is a two-way process wherein the consulted are active participants in the process of creating a consensus that legitimizes public-policy decisions. The real test for both councils, therefore, will be the degree to which their members actually participate in the process (shura) or devolve into a mere sounding board or rubber stamp for government policies (tashawir). Regardless of the future of the Majlis, however, as an adaptation of a classical Islamic concept to modern government, it reflects remarkable vision and creativity by its creator, King Fahd.

THE SAUDI POLITICAL PROCESS

The Saudi political process basically operates on three levels: royal family politics, national politics, and bureaucratic politics. All are separate but interrelated.

Royal Family Politics

The Al Saud family comprises the main constituency of the kingdom, and without its support no king can be chosen or maintain power. Technically, this support is granted and withdrawn by an old Islamic institution, *ahl al-hall wal-'uqd* (the people who bind and loose), and requires a fatwa to give it legality. In fact, however, the royal family dominates this institution. (Other members include religious leaders, technocrats, businessmen, and heads of important families not otherwise mentioned previously.)

Saudi royal succession was marked by intrigue and violence during its first 150 years, and many Western observers believe that it still constitutes a major threat to Saudi internal stability.[12] Since the creation of the kingdom by Abd al-Aziz in 1932, however, royal succession has been relatively orderly, passing to Abd al-Aziz's sons by seniority and in accordance with the Islamic law.

In 1933, Abd al-Aziz formally named his oldest surviving son, Saud, as heir apparent. The king also made clear that his next oldest surviving son, Faysal, should succeed Saud, thus creating the tradition that succession should pass down among his sons. Sixty years later, King Fahd formalized the succession process in the Basic Law of Government of 1992, which provided for succession to pass to the sons of King Abd al-Aziz and their sons. The Basic Law stipulated that the king would name his heir apparent and could also relieve him by royal decree.

This move was obviously an attempt to avoid disruptive political infighting within the family in choosing a new ruler. Some claimed, however, that by formally granting the right of the king to remove an heir apparent, Fahd made the process more capricious.[13] In fact, naming an heir apparent must be based on the prior consensus of the royal family. If such a consensus is difficult to obtain, royal family politicking will be virtually certain to occur no matter what formal regulations are in force.

In the near term, royal succession does not appear to be a major problem. There are several sons of King Abd al-Aziz who are qualified to rule. Older but less qualified brothers might contest the naming of an heir apparent and might even hold out for some type of compensation for not being chosen, but it is doubtful that they could get a consensus and obtain the position themselves. Because choosing an heir apparent must be one of the first priorities of a new ruler in order to preserve stability, it seems unlikely that royal family politicking among the sons of Abd al-Aziz will be allowed to reach crisis proportions. Moreover, once a consensus on an heir apparent is reached, it would be infinitely more difficult to create a new consensus to remove him.

When no more qualified brothers are available, the question of succession could present difficulties. There are not only scores of grandsons of King Abd al-Aziz, but many of them are well educated and experienced in public service and none apparently has an inside track to rulership. Royal family politicking in choosing an heir apparent from among the grandsons could thus become intense. Nevertheless, given that the future survival of the regime depends on reaching a consensus on an heir apparent from the new generation when the time comes, it is difficult to conceive that the family will not coalesce around a candidate.

Not surprisingly, royal family politics revolve around ijma "and shura— consultation and consensus. Yet little is known outside the family about how this process actually operates. The family is large (an estimated 3,000 to 10,000 princes) and has historically been rife with rivalries and contention. Nevertheless, it assiduously shuns publicity and always seeks to maintain an outward appearance of unanimity.

Within the family, factors such as branch, generation, seniority, and sibling ties are very important, particularly in the case of Abd al-Aziz's sons by the same mother. (He had numerous wives, although—by Islamic law—no more than four at a time). The ruling branch consists of the descendants of Abd al-Aziz's father, and succession is assumed to be limited to the sons of Abd al-Aziz and their male offspring. Because he had many sons, some are actually younger than their nephews, but the latter are of a more junior generation and hence generally less influential.

There are various collateral branches of the family descended from brothers of former rulers. Two of the leading collateral branches are the Saud al-Kabirs, who descend from an older brother of Abd al-Rahman, and the Ibn Jaluwis, who descend from Abd al-Rahman's uncle, Jaluwi. Technically, the head of the Saud al-Kabir branch outranks all but the king because its founder was an elder brother of Abd al-Rahman, but in fact the Abd al-Aziz branch has a monopoly of influence. Another collateral branch, the Thunayans, are descended from a brother of the founder of the dynasty and lived for many years in Turkey. King Faysal's wife 'Iffat was descended from this branch. In time, the ruling branch will undoubtedly produce additional collateral branches.

Among the sons of Abd al-Aziz, seniority of birth is important but not absolute in determining influence. Older princes not deemed capable of maintaining positions of influence are excluded from the decision-making process except for purely royal family business. Finally, sons of the same mother tend to act collectively. The most powerful sibling group is King Fahd and his six full brothers, sometimes called the "Sudayri Seven" after their mother, the late Hussa bint al-Sudayri, or Al Fahd (Family of Fahd), after Fahd, the eldest brother. They include Prince Sultan, Prince Salman, Prince Naif, and Prince Ahmad.

The Al Saud maintains through family politics its primary role as the political constituency of the kingdom, and the ruler must have its collective support to be appointed and continue in power. With family standing based on seniority, senior princes generally have more leverage in royal family politics than junior princes. As a result, uncles often attempt to use their royal family seniority to override nephews of equal or even greater government seniority on government policy issues. This practice tends to blur the lines between royal family politics and national politics.

National Politics

The Saudi Council of Ministers has thus far never played a strong role in national government; national political issues are still decided to a great extent by the traditional, personalized methods of the past. The difference is that, with the decline in the influence of personal retainers in the royal diwan, the consultation process today is increasingly directed to those with professional expertise—technocrats. Moreover, with the rapid expansion of more formal governmental institutions and insistence on appointment of technocrats in appropriate ministries, senior officials from cabinet minister on down are increasingly consulted on the basis of their official responsibilities rather than simply their personal ties to the ruler.

One of the primary means of maintaining coherence in the national political arena is the budget process. Each ministry and independent agency must submit an annual budget and compete for funding. With overall spending reduced since the free-wheeling days of the 1970s oil boom, the competition can be fierce. Spending priorities are based to some degree on long-term planning and short-term necessity, but by and large the budget process is a free-for-all. At worst, it distorts true priorities; at best, it provides competition that can help weed out marginal budget requests.

Most of the top national security positions and major provincial governorships in the kingdom are held by royal family members. Most of them are younger brothers of the king; however, several next-generation princes (grandsons of Abd al-Aziz) and members of collateral branches also have positions of influence. Although the royal family holds many of the senior positions in government, the regime has always realized the need for technocrats and has made sure that government positions requiring professional expertise, both military and civilian, are filled with qualified people. Most of the ministries requiring a high order of professional or administrative expertise are held by such people. The senior technocrats have considerable powers both as principal advisors to the king in their areas of responsibility, and as operational decision makers. Virtually all major policy decisions involve some configuration of technocrats and senior royal family members. One should not forget, however, that the technocrats function as professionals in the policy-making process rather than as independent politicians.

In recent years, an increasing number of young Western-educated royal family members, including those from collateral branches, have entered government and begun to rise in the ranks of the bureaucracy, creating a new category, royal technocrats. Each year, however, as more senior positions are occupied, the younger princes join the government in more junior positions. It is still too soon to see how they will ultimately affect the equation, but so far the most successful have won respect on merit as much as rank.

Bureaucratic Politics

It is difficult to assess the degree of centralization in the decision-making process in national politics. The king certainly has more power than his predecessors, owing to the accumulation of oil wealth. He is the head of a government that is increasingly intruding into the lives of the citizens through its control of national wealth. If there were an archetypal rentier state (a state whose economy is dominated by publicly owned fixed income—in this case, oil income), Saudi Arabia could certainly qualify.

At the same time, as the government has expanded rapidly over the years, the sheer size and complexity of government operations have made it impossible for the king to be personally involved in all but the most pressing national issues requiring a decision. For lesser decisions, the locus of power is quite often at the ministry or agency level. Because of a general tendency toward personalization of politics and because many of the ministries predate the founding of the Saudi Council of Ministers, there is often keen competition among them for resources and a great deal of overlapping responsibility. All the ministries are highly independent, and bureaucratic infighting among them can be fierce. On the other hand, responsibilities for given areas can be assigned to officials from other ministries as a result of personal preferences, political influence, and force of habit. For example, Prince Sultan, the defense minister, has for years had a supervisory role over Saudi-Yemeni relations, even though they are nominally a Foreign Ministry responsibility.

Ministries and agencies jealously guard their prerogatives. For instance, they tend to have a proprietary attitude toward Western companies contracted to perform services for them. It is seldom that a firm with a major contract with one ministry can be successful in bidding on a major contract with another ministry, particularly without the first ministry's tacit consent.

In general, the evolution of public administration in Saudi Arabia has consisted of a gradual shift from the traditional rule of King Abd al-Aziz to a more institutionalized, bureaucratized government. The creation of a government bureaucracy, however, has not greatly diminished the high degree of personalization in the decision-making process. Delegation of authority through an established chain of command is still very weak, and even the most trivial decisions are often made by a handful of men at senior levels. Nevertheless, personalized politics have been rechanneled from the traditional system to the present bureaucratic structure, and it is within that structure that bureaucratic politics have grown and flourished in Saudi Arabia. Bureaucratic procedures have become increasingly important in decision making and constitute a growing constraint on arbitrary and capricious policies.

With the expansion of government operations, the bureaucracy has also developed as an important means of participation in the political process. Senior bureaucrats, including commoners, can wield extraordinary power, at least in an operational sense. For many years, this acted as an important brake to rising demands for more political participation. With almost no room for expansion, however, and with many positions held by relatively young men who can reasonably be expected to remain in government for many years, access to political participation through the bureaucracy is increasingly being denied to younger-generation Saudis. Moves to expand political participation, therefore, have come at an opportune time.

4

Oil and Saudi Arabia

By any standards, Saudi Arabia is the most important oil-producing state in the world today. It has more than one-fourth of the world's oil reserves, and with the breakup of the Soviet Union and a sharp decline in former-Soviet production, it has become the world's largest oil producer. At the end of 1993, Saudi Arabia produced slightly more than 8 million barrels of oil per day (mbd), which, with Iraqi production closed in, accounted for roughly one-third of total Organization of Petroleum Exporting States (OPEC) production.[1] It is also the world's third largest producer of natural gas.

In 1992, oil revenues exceeded $54 billion, of which more than $45 billion were foreign sales. Oil revenues make up about 40 percent of the Saudi gross national product (GNP) but, more important, about 80 percent of government receipts. About 90 percent of total export earnings are oil-related. At the same time, only about 2 percent of the Saudi labor force is employed in the oil industry, of which about 85 percent are Saudis.

The Making of an Oil Kingdom: 1901–1967

With these figures, it is easy to see why Saudi Arabia is perceived as the quintessential Arab oil kingdom. Far more difficult to realize is that just a few decades ago it was one of the poorest countries on earth. The story of how a remote desert principality developed into a modern oil kingdom begins at the turn of the twentieth century, before the creation of Saudi Arabia itself.

On May 28, 1901, William Knox D'Arcy, a British financier who had made a fortune in gold mine speculation in Australia, concluded an oil concession agreement with the Shah of Persia that was soon to usher in a new oil age in the Middle East. It would also make Great Britain the preeminent oil power in the region for two-thirds of the twentieth century. From the concession emerged the Anglo-Persian Oil Company, later renamed Anglo-Iranian (AIOC) and ultimately British Petroleum (BP).

The oil business was far different then than it is today. The petroleum product in greatest demand in the nineteenth century was kerosene. With natural

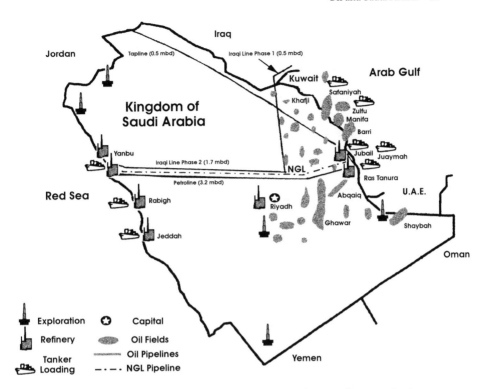

Map 3. Saudi oil installations, oil fields, refineries, pipelines, and terminals. *Source:* International Energy Agency.

gas, it was used for heating and cooking and, in the industrial world, for lighting. Just when Thomas Edison's invention of the incandescent light bulb in 1877 appeared to deprive petroleum of its greatest long-term market, a new market opened up with the invention of the internal combustion engine. In the United States, in particular, this was to change the entire culture into one literally driven by the automobile.

Although the automobile age was still far off in the early 1900s, oil-fired engines were finding other uses. One of the most momentous decisions for Middle East oil was the British decision in 1912 to henceforth propel its navy by oil instead of coal. That change almost instantly made Middle East oil a strategic commodity; and when War World I broke out two years later, the importance of oil as a strategic material was assured.

Although the British obtained the first Middle East oil concessions, it was the Americans who developed Saudi oil resources. In the early years, however, the U.S.-Saudi oil relationship was far from certain. Before World War I, the Americans, who were already the world's leading oil producers and net exporters, showed little interest in obtaining foreign concessions. The war briefly spurred official interest in foreign oil as a strategic reserve because U.S. allies, cut off from their own sources, had become largely dependent on the United States.[2] The Middle East appeared to be one of the most promising areas for American companies.

Official U.S. interest in Middle East oil continued in the 1920s, not so much from a concern for strategic reserves as from the desire to ensure that U.S. oil companies were not prevented by their European competitors from obtaining oil concessions. With strong government encouragement, seven U.S. oil companies created a joint venture called the Near East Development Company. The original companies were Standard Oil of New Jersey (Exxon), Standard Oil of New York (Mobil), Gulf, the Texas Company (Texaco), Sinclair, Atlantic Oil Company (now part of Atlantic-Richfield [ARCO]), and Pan American Petroleum (Standard Oil of Indiana). By the time of the acquisition, Texaco and Sinclair had dropped out, and the shares of Pan American and Atlantic had been purchased by Standard of New Jersey and Standard of New York. Backed by the State Department, the joint venture obtained a 23.75 percent interest in the Iraq Petroleum Company (IPC) in July 1928.[3] The other owners of IPC were Anglo-Persian, Royal Dutch Shell, and French interests, each of which owned 23.75 percent. Calouste Gulbenkian, the Armenian oil man who before World War I had put together IPC's predecessor, the Turkish Petroleum Company, retained a 5 percent equity for which he was nicknamed "Mr. Five Percent."

As it turned out, a far more important holdover from the old Turkish Petroleum Company was a self-denial clause retained by IPC. This clause stipulated that none of the owners would undertake oil operations in an area that included most of the former Ottoman Empire except in cooperation with the other owners. Gulbenkian later claimed that he redefined that area in 1928 by drawing a line with a red pencil around the defunct Ottoman Empire, including Asia Minor, the Fertile Crescent, and all of Arabia except for Kuwait. True or not, the clause became known as the Red Line Agreement, and it included Saudi Arabia.[4]

By 1928, the sense of urgency about acquiring foreign supplies that had motivated both the U.S. government and U.S. oil companies to look for Middle East oil concessions in the early 1920s had disappeared. Worldwide overcapacity and overproduction had become more immediate problems. Many officials in both business and government feared that the financial stability of the entire oil industry could be jeopardized if the search for new markets led to cutthroat competition and price wars.

Accordingly, in September 1928, just two months after the IPC agreement, the chief executive officers of Royal Dutch Shell, Anglo-Persian, Jersey Standard, Gulf, and Standard of Indiana met at Achnacarry Castle in Scotland, ostensibly for grouse shooting but in reality to hammer out a formula for limiting free competition and allocating market shares. The As Is Agreement, as it came to be called, and the Red Line Agreement were among the first successful attempts to cartelize the international oil industry. Thus, the motivating force behind creating an international oil cartel was not to raise prices, as was later popularly assumed, but to prevent them from collapsing. With the onset of the Great Depression just a year away, the international oil cartel became even more of a myth as the oil companies desperately sought to expand their dwindling markets worldwide at the expense of their competitors.

As demand declined due to the depression and supply continued to expand with new finds, U.S. government interest in foreign oil supplies declined precipitously in the 1930s. Ironically, it was during this period of minimal government involvement in Middle East oil that U.S. oil companies became established in Saudi Arabia. One might argue that the lack of official support helped the companies more than it hurt them in obtaining a Saudi oil concession. Of all the competing companies, only those from the United States were not suspected by King Abd al-Aziz of being the precursors of imperial political interests.[5]

The Americans were not the first to be interested in a Saudi oil concession. In 1923, Major Frank Holmes, an entrepreneur and adventurer from New Zealand, obtained a concession for his Near Eastern and General Syndicate to explore for oil. Holmes was aided in persuading Abd al-Aziz (then sultan of Nadj) to grant the concession by a Lebanese-American, Ameen Rihani. Although Abd al-Aziz was wary of opening up his country to foreign political exploitation, he was chronically in need of money, which an oil concession could provide. Moreover, he did not really believe that Holmes would find oil, a view commonly held by many oil geologists of the day, who believed that Saudi geology was not favorable for oil discovery.

Holmes was never really interested in searching for oil but in selling his concession to a company that was. He found no takers, and in 1928 the concession lapsed. In the meantime, he had negotiated another concession with the amirate of Bahrain, which he promptly sold to Gulf Oil Corporation. Because Gulf was bound by the Red Line Agreement, however, it was not able to exploit the concession and sold it in turn to Standard Oil of California (Socal, now Chevron). There was one more complication. Bahrain had signed an agreement with Britain permitting only British or British Commonwealth companies to explore for oil. Socal got around this restriction by creating a wholly owned Canadian subsidiary, the Bahrain Petroleum Company (Bapco); and in 1932 Bapco struck oil.

The Bahrain archipelago is located only forty kilometers off the Saudi coast. (They are now linked by a causeway.) Finding oil so close to the mainland revived interest among Socal geologists in exploring for oil in Saudi Arabia; and with the help of H. St. John B. Philby and Karl Twitchell, Socal persuaded King Abd al-Aziz to grant the company an oil concession. Philby was a British army officer, diplomat, and adventurer who had met Abd al-Aziz on an official mission during World War I and stayed on to become a close advisor. Twitchell was an American engineer who had previously surveyed Saudi water and mineral resources and was trusted by the king. The concession agreement was concluded in May 1933 and ratified by royal decree during the following July. In September, the first oil prospectors stepped ashore at Jubayl, then a small village but now a major petrochemical industrial center and site of a Saudi naval base. In November 1933, Socal placed the concession under another wholly owned subsidiary, the California Arabian Standard Oil Company (Casoc), the precursor of Aramco.[6]

Drilling commenced on April 30, 1935. The first well, called Dammam No. 1, and five subsequent wells were drilled to the same depth at which oil had been discovered in Bahrain; but the results were disappointing, with no oil found in commercial quantities. Therefore, when Dammam No. 7 was spudded in on December 7, 1936, drilling continued below the Bahrain zone. On March 3, 1938, Dammam No. 7 began producing more than 1,500 barrels per day (b/d)—compared to between five and ten b/d for many wells in the United States—and has done so ever since. Saudi Arabia had entered the oil age.

With world markets both politically and economically disrupted by the world economic depression and the deteriorating political situation that ultimately led to World War II, the 1930s were not the best of times for bringing new oil discoveries onstream. Thus, the kingdom had to wait until the end of World War II before any significant Saudi oil exports were made or revenues accrued. In the meantime, Socal was endeavoring to negotiate with other oil companies to prevent a collapse in prices resulting from Saudi and Bahraini oil's coming onstream. The problem was solved, not through negotiations but by selling half-equity in both operations to Texaco. Texaco had overseas markets and almost no overseas oil, whereas Socal had few overseas markets and an abundance of overseas oil. In 1936, the two companies combined Near East and Asian operations, including Casoc and Bapco, under a jointly owned subsidiary named the California Texas Oil Company, or Caltex. Texaco in turn purchased half-interest in Casoc for $3 million plus $18 million in deferred equity.

Unfortunately for King Abd al-Aziz, the deteriorating political and economic conditions of the 1930s placed him in even greater financial straits than had chronically been the case. Saudi Arabia's economy depended primarily on Hajj receipts; and as the numbers of Hajjis dropped either from economic distress or because political conditions made international travel impossible, Saudi Arabia's financial situation neared collapse.

Initially, Casoc tried to keep Abd al-Aziz economically afloat through loans and advances on future revenues; but in early 1941, believing it could no longer afford to do so, Casoc appealed to the U.S. government to help bail out the king. Although the United States had not yet entered the war, many government officials believed that it would ultimately be drawn in, and interest in the strategic value of oil supplies was renewed. Therefore, they were favorably disposed to helping out the kingdom. Nevertheless, two years of protracted debate ensued within the U.S. government, in addition to U.S. negotiations with Saudi Arabia and Britain (considered the preeminent political power in the region), before help was on the way.

Help took the form of a declaration on February 18, 1943 by U.S. Secretary of State Cordell Hull, who said that Saudi Arabia was eligible for U.S. Lend Lease aid. By extending aid through the Lend Lease program, which was justified on strategic military grounds, the United States not only ensured that Saudi Arabia would remain financially solvent during the war but entered into military cooperation with the kingdom that has been a major element in U.S.-Saudi relations ever since.[7]

As had happened in World War I, official U.S. interest in the strategic importance of Saudi oil soared during World War II; similarly, it declined after the war. In 1943, U.S. Secretary of the Interior Harold Ickes recommended that the government purchase all, or at least part, of Casoc. There was certainly sufficient precedent in Europe for such a move, but in the United States Casoc's owners successfully opposed government equity on the grounds of traditional nongovernment involvement in private business. Nevertheless, the strategic importance of oil did convince both U.S. businessmen and public officials that, because of oil's strategic importance, some form of government involvement in foreign oil operations was inevitable.

By 1948, U.S. interest in Middle East oil had again waned, and the government reverted to a policy of passive support for private U.S. oil companies operating in the region. Casoc's owners were left to work out for themselves such problems as market shares with their European and other American competitors.

The end of the war enabled Saudi oil to enter the market in significant quantities. Again, however, Aramco's owners (Casoc's name had officially been changed to the Arabian American Oil Company on January 31, 1944) became concerned about the effect of such an increase in supply on world oil prices. Fearing that the entry of so much oil on a glutted postwar international market could lead to price wars and a collapse of the entire market (a concern that

Figure 16. Saudi
Aramco oil derrick.
Photo by Saudi
Aramco.

had led to the creation of Casoc in the first place), they attempted to acquire
additional partners in Aramco with worldwide marketing operations that could
distribute Aramco's production more widely.

The two most logical choices were Jersey Standard and Standard of New
York. Both had limited Middle East operations (they shared in the 23.75 percent American equity in IPC), and both had worldwide downstream (refining
and marketing) operations. But both were signatories to the Red Line Agreement prohibiting them from developing upstream oil resources in Arabia without sharing with the other signatories. With strong support from the U.S. government, the obstacles to obtaining equity in Aramco were overcome (which
included setting aside the Red Line Agreement), and in December 1948 Jersey
Standard purchased 30 percent and Standard of New York 10 percent of Aramco.

The two original owners, Standard of California and Texaco, each retained a 30 percent equity.

There was still no thought on the part of the oil-producing countries at this time to seek state ownership of their oil resources. King Abd al-Aziz in particular wanted a wholly U.S. concession, which he thought would remain a solely commercial venture and not become an instrument of politics. The king never tired of seeking better financial terms from concessionaires, however. Thus, in 1949, he granted a concession to J. Paul Getty's Pacific Western Oil Corporation (later Getty Oil Company) in the Saudi-Kuwaiti neutral zone, which gave the kingdom far better terms than it had obtained from Aramco. (The neutral zone had been created by the British in 1920 to accommodate the Bedouins who roamed the area between the two countries and for whom fixed boundaries made little sense. Both Kuwait and Saudi Arabia agreed to administer the territory jointly and share oil production developed there.)

In 1950, Saudi Arabia began to pressure Aramco for better terms as well. After intense negotiations, the company agreed to 50–50 net profit sharing, with royalties and Saudi taxes credited to the Saudi share. A major obstacle to the agreement was Aramco's fears that it would be subject to double taxation—to both Saudi Arabia and the United States. This problem was overcome when the U.S. Treasury Department subsequently ruled that Aramco would be granted a tax exemption on the profit sharing, which in effect exempted

Figure 17. Saudi Aramco oil rig, Rubʿ al-Khali. Photo by Saudi Aramco.

the company from paying U.S. taxes. The transfer of the tax liability to the United States was later cited by critics of the oil industry as a devious backroom deal, but there is no doubt that Aramco's owners took great pains to make sure that the entire agreement was drafted in strict accordance with U.S. tax laws.[8]

The Saudis were soon to do even better than 50–50, however. In 1957, a Japanese consortium, the Arabian Oil Company (AOC), was created to seek an offshore concession in the neutral zone. AOC agreed to a 44–56 split in the Saudis' favor, which was later increased to 43–57 when AOC agreed to those terms with Kuwait. Furthermore, when AOC discovered oil in 1960, Saudi Arabia and Kuwait took a 10 percent equity share in the company.

THE RISE OF OPEC: 1967–1973

By 1967, Saudi Arabia was well established as a major oil producer. Yet despite its growing wealth and status, it was internationally one of the least known and understood members of the major oil-producing states. Events soon transpired, however, to make both Saudi Arabia and OPEC (the producer cartel that the kingdom came to dominate) household words.

Despite U.S. Interior Secretary Ickes's dire warnings during World War II that the United States would become a net importer of oil, new worldwide postwar discoveries perpetuated a world market glut right through the 1960s. The major oil companies maintained price stability through collusion in regulating production rates. When a soft market indicated that production cuts were necessary to keep the price of oil from collapsing, however, the revenues of the producing countries were reduced drastically. In 1960, Venezuela, twice stung by drastic production cuts unilaterally imposed by the oil companies, sought to organize the producing countries to speak with one voice against such company decisions. Thus, in September 1960, OPEC was born. Saudi Arabia, which had also been stung, gave its full cooperation.

At the time, OPEC had virtually no influence over oil prices, in large part because the continuing oil glut perpetuated a buyer's market. Moreover, the producers were keenly aware of Iran's experience a decade earlier. In 1951, Iran, then the world's largest exporter, nationalized its oil resources in the belief that the world could not get along without its oil and, in a spate of anti-Western nationalism, did not offer due compensation to the concessionaire, AIOC. Unfortunately for Iran, there was more than enough oil production elsewhere to meet world demand; and in the resulting dispute over compensation with AIOC, Iran was forced to cease production until it reached a settlement that was far more generous than the Iranians had wished. Moreover, it never recovered its position as the number one oil-exporting nation.

The glut continued over the next two decades, and during that period the producing companies seemed to hold all the cards. Nevertheless, with the creation of OPEC, the idea had been planted among the oil-producing countries that one day they would gain control of their own oil resources.[9]

Structural changes were taking place in the world economy at this time that would end the glut. Throughout the 1960s, world oil demand rose faster than supply. In Europe, industries were changing from coal to oil at a rate faster than predicted; and in the United States, already the world's greatest oil consumer, cheap oil prices boosted demand even more. Oil consumption was also on the rise throughout the Third World.

The end of the glut came in 1970 and was helped by the fact that the United States had for the first time become a net importer of oil. The shift to a seller's market enabled the producing countries to supplant the oil companies in setting price and production rates and then finally to gain complete ownership over their own oil and gas resources.

In retrospect, the process actually began with the June 1967 Arab-Israeli war. By closing the Suez Canal, the war created a tanker shortage and placed a premium on Libyan crude, which did not have to transit the canal and was also valued for its low sulphur content. In response, Libya demanded a price increase. Negotiations began in September 1969, the same month that a group of Libyan army officers under Colonel Muʿammar Qadhafi seized power. The Libyans concentrated on Occidental Petroleum, a small "independent" U.S. oil company with few sources of crude outside Libya, and demanded that it agree to pay them higher revenues or face nationalization. Occidental tried to resist the Libyan demands by seeking alternative crude supplies from the major oil companies, but the majors, not realizing the folly of their actions, summarily turned down Occidental's request. It therefore had no alternative but to give in, and in August 1970 signed an agreement giving Libya a 20 percent increase in oil royalties and tax revenues. By December, all the other companies in Libya, including the major oil companies, were also forced to capitulate.[10]

The Libyan victory heralded a new era for international oil as other OPEC countries quickly demanded higher prices and tax rates. At a meeting in Tehran in February 1971, oil companies operating in the Gulf signed an agreement with their host governments agreeing to terms similar to those obtained by Libya. This agreement marked the transfer of control over oil price and production-rate setting from the oil companies to the oil-producing countries in OPEC.

At the same time, the oil-producing countries were acquiring ownership of the oil resources that the companies had previously owned through the concession agreements. Most countries accomplished this by nationalization. Three countries—Saudi Arabia, Qatar, and the United Arab Emirates—did so through "participation," a scheme first developed by then Saudi petroleum minister, Ahmad Zaki Yamani, in a speech at the American University of Beirut in 1967.

Yamani subsequently explained the participation idea to U.S. Ambassador Hermann Eilts and some of his staff at a meeting at Yamani's summer house near Ta'if. At the time, most oil industry experts dismissed the idea, not realizing the great changes in store in the next few years.

Yamani believed that direct nationalization of oil resources held certain disadvantages, including the negative political associations of punitive nationalization schemes. More important, he feared the prospect of cutthroat competition among the oil-producing countries for market shares, leading to a collapse of the market—the same fear that the companies had expressed at Achnacarry Castle some forty years earlier.

As an alternative, he proposed allowing the companies to maintain equity in upstream (production) operations for a period of time during which they would participate as partners in maintaining market stability. This concept was subsequently endorsed by OPEC in June 1968, and in July 1971 the organization passed a resolution calling for its immediate implementation.

After extensive bargaining, Saudi Arabia, Qatar, and the United Arab Emirates concluded participation agreements with the major concessionaires in late 1972. The kingdom acquired 25 percent ownership of Aramco early the next year and in doing so established control over Aramco company policy. It was therefore in no hurry to complete the process of buying out the company's equity. It increased its share to 60 percent in 1974 and finally to 100 percent in 1980. The new national oil company's name was changed to Saudi Aramco. It is interesting to note that the neutral zone concessionaires, Getty (now owned by Texaco) and AOC, were not affected by participation and have maintained their concessions.

THE ARAB OIL EMBARGO: 1973–1974

As we have seen, market forces—not political forces—determine the price of oil in the long run. When the oil glut of the 1950s and 1960s finally gave way to a shortage, it set the stage for the precipitous price rises of the 1970s. Within this broad economic context, however, short-term political disruptions did have a profound effect on the market. As noted earlier, the 1967 Arab-Israeli war created an oil tanker shortage that contributed to the transfer of control over oil production from the oil companies to the producing countries. The 1967 war was not the sole cause of the transfer of control, but it did serve as a catalyst, causing the transfer to occur sooner rather than later.

The 1973 Arab-Israeli war had a far greater disruptive effect on the market in the form of the Arab oil embargo. The Arab oil-producing states had attempted an embargo during the 1967 war, but it failed due to world-wide spare production capacity at the time. By 1973, the oil market had changed completely; and with a world shortage, the oil embargo was extremely effective.

In September 1973, OPEC demanded higher oil prices in response to an increasingly tight market. When negotiations with the oil companies convened in Vienna on October 8 to agree on a price, OPEC demanded a 100 percent increase. The companies, powerless to resist, broke off negotiations; and on October 16, the Gulf producers met in Kuwait and unilaterally raised posted prices 70 percent.

In the meantime, the 1973 Arab-Israeli war had broken out on October 6. For almost a year before the war, King Faysal had been warning anyone who would listen that, unless some progress were made on a Middle East peace settlement, the Arabs would be forced to use oil as political leverage to offset one-sided U.S. support for Israel. They believed such support enabled the Israelis to continue to deny Palestinians their right of self-determination.

When the war broke out, President Nixon personally assured King Faysal that the United States intended to remain evenhanded during the fighting and would strive to establish a cease-fire. Therefore, when on October 19 Nixon asked Congress for $2.2 billion in military aid to Israel, Faysal considered the request not only gratuitous but a betrayal of the president's personal assurances to him. The following day, under the aegis of the Organization of Arab Petroleum Exporting Countries (OAPEC), Faysal instituted the oil embargo.[11]

The embargo had two parts: an absolute embargo on the United States and the Netherlands, considered especially friendly to Israel, and a cutback in production to ensure that the embargoed countries could not simply shift purchasing patterns for a fungible worldwide product—that is, increase imports from non-Arab sources whose customers would then increase purchases from Arab sources. To make it all work, the Saudis threatened to cut off Saudi oil supplies to Aramco's owners—four of the world's seven major oil companies—unless they geared their international supply networks to deny Arab oil to the Americans and the Dutch. The embargo was highly effective; and the artificial shortage it created was quickly exploited by OPEC price hawks, led by Iran to again increase prices. At the December OPEC meeting, posted oil prices were raised another 130 percent.[12]

The embargo, which lasted until March 1974, was essentially an economic response to a political problem and should therefore be seen as political policy rather than oil policy. In the United States, the embargo-induced oil shortage (exacerbated by inept U.S. policies) was met with surprise and outrage. In retrospect, no one should have been surprised that the Saudis and other Arab producers would attempt to extract a political price for U.S. Middle East policies that were considered even by moderate Arabs to be hostile to their interests. They used virtually the only form of leverage on U.S. policies they had—oil.

Despite all the hysteria among consumer countries over the embargo, it had relatively little lasting impact on the Arab-Israeli problem other than to make Saudi Arabia anathema to Israel and its supporters. They feared that the West and particularly the United States might "sell out Israel for a barrel of Saudi oil." The embargo had a far greater impact on the oil market, exacerbating the oil shortage and resulting in high prices for much of 1970s. The high prices in turn forced consumers to become more energy-efficient and search for not only other sources of oil but also non-oil sources of energy. It also led to the creation of the International Energy Agency by major consuming countries in an attempt to work collectively to avoid another panic situation if oil were again used as a political weapon.

From the Saudi point of view, the embargo was not an unqualified success. With few natural resources other than oil and gas, the Saudis have always favored stable prices low enough to ensure a long-term market for their oil and discourage shifts to nonfossil fuels. It has deviated from this policy only when short-term political or economic circumstances dictate. The 1973 Arab-Israeli war was such a circumstance. Ironically, the economic impact of the embargo was contrary to Saudi long-term economic interests. Not only did the embargo spur energy conservation and a worldwide search for alternative sources of energy, but the soaring oil prices of the 1970s, which enabled the Saudis to amass billions of dollars in foreign exchange, led to a deeper and longer glut in the 1980s that ultimately saw those reserves disappear.

THE PERIOD OF OPEC ASCENDANCY: 1974–1990

The Arab oil embargo underscored the completion of the process that had begun in the late 1960s, when OPEC countries seized control of their own oil resources and acquired the ability to set price and production rates worldwide. Within OPEC, Saudi Arabia emerged as uncontested leader. From a backward desert principality, it became the most important country controlling one of the world's most important commodities.

In many respects, few of OPEC's successes in the 1970s were of its own making. OPEC was not the monolithic cartel that it has been described. Its actions required unanimity that was very hard to get. There was a fundamental split between "price moderates" such as Saudi Arabia, which had few other natural resources and saw its interests best served by moderate prices and long-term market stability, and "price hawks" such as Iran and Algeria, which saw their interests best served by high prices and high revenues to be used for rapid economic development.

What kept OPEC together, other than a strong desire by all its members for its continued existence, was the fact that most OPEC states were already producing at near capacity; thus, maintaining market shares was not a problem. The Saudis, who produced far more oil than their revenue needs required, could afford to raise or lower production to maintain price stability. Being the "swing producer" became a basic tenet of Saudi oil policy. Under Saudi leadership, the absolute price of oil actually dropped during this period. (That is, the rise in prices was less than the rise in inflation.) In late 1976, Saudi Arabia and the United Arab Emirates even broke ranks with the rest of OPEC, increasing oil prices only 5 percent compared to 10 percent for the others. In the summer of 1977, the two countries raised their prices an additional 5 percent in return for a price freeze that was maintained until the end of 1979.[13]

The Oil Glut of the 1980s

In the summer of 1978, the Middle East was again on the way toward another political disruption of the oil market—the Iranian revolution. By December, it became clear even to a previously optimistic U.S. government that the shah's regime was in very serious trouble. When Ayatallah Khomeini returned to Iran from exile in February 1979, the end was in sight. He quickly organized an interim government and, following a plebescite, announced the creation of an Islamic republic on April 1, 1980.

The fall of the shah had a psychological impact on the market similar to the one the Arab embargo had made six years earlier, sending spot oil prices soaring. Fears that Iranian oil would stay off the market due to political upheavals were largely unfounded; but panic buying continued, further encouraged by strategic stockpiling. Having been caught with few strategic reserves in 1973, many countries and companies had planned extra storage capacity for just such a contingency. The added pressure of stockpiling on oil demand helped drive up oil prices even higher, from around $25 per barrel in early 1979 to over $40 by mid-1980.

In September 1980, the market faced yet another political disruption, the outbreak of the Iran-Iraq war. This time, however, the results were not the same as in 1973 or 1979. The price of oil was already inflated beyond its true market value, and worldwide recessionary trends were beginning to lower prices. After a brief spike following the outbreak of the war, prices continued to decline. The oil glut of the 1980s was setting in.

Being swing producer in the 1980s brought the Saudis none of the benefits of the 1970s, for the glut was not solely the result of recession. World oil-production capacity had also increased greatly. The seller's market of the 1970s had set off a worldwide search for oil, and high prices made additional oil supplies commercially viable that formerly were too expensive to extract. Thus, as demand declined due to recession, OPEC's market share declined even more. In addition, energy conservation during the years of high prices had proved

Table 1. Crude Oil Production, 1973–1995 (in millions of barrels per day)

Year	Saudi Arabia	OPEC	World
1973	7.6	31.0	58.1
1974	8.5	30.7	58.2
1975	7.1	27.2	55.3
1976	8.6	30.7	59.7
1977	9.2	31.9	62.0
1978	8.3	29.9	63.3
1979	9.6	31.0	65.8
1980	9.9	26.0	62.9
1981	9.8	22.7	59.3
1982	6.5	19.3	56.6
1983	5.0	17.8	56.5
1984	4.6	17.5	57.7
1985	3.4	16.6	58.9
1986	5.0	18.6	59.9
1987	4.2	18.3	59.9
1988	5.2	20.4	62.3
1989	5.2	22.6	63.8
1990	6.5	22.7	67.0
1991	8.2	22.7	66.6
1992	8.4	24.0	67.1
1993	8.1	24.7	67.3
1994	8.1	25.1	68.6
1995	8.2	25.5	68.8

Source: Petroleum Finance Company, Washington, D.C..

far more effective than anticipated because the consuming countries had learned to be much more energy-efficient. The increased supply and reduced per capita consumption further accelerated the swing to a buyer's market.

At the same time, the OPEC countries had adjusted their national budgets to match their higher revenues; and when the decline in prices set in, they were politically unable to reduce their expenditures as rapidly as revenues declined. Despite agreement to cut production proportionately, the overwhelming temptation was to maintain revenue levels by pumping as much oil as possible. The Saudis, as swing producer, were forced to cut production to maintain price stability. Saudi production thus dropped from 9.8 mbd in 1981 to a low of 2.34 mbd for August 1985.

For the Saudis, maintaining the position of swing producer was untenable. Although they were confident that demand would eventually pick up, their revenues in mid-1985 were less than half of their budgetary expenditures. As a result, they again increased production, causing prices to drop briefly below $10 per barrel in 1986 but ultimately forcing other OPEC producers to share the burden of production cuts to stabilize prices and regain lost market share. OPEC discipline could not be maintained, however, and in 1988 Saudi Arabia again increased production and collapsed prices. The influence of OPEC was at its lowest ebb in fifteen years.

The Iraqi Invasion of Kuwait

Yet another major political disruption of the oil market occurred in August 1990 when Iraqi troops invaded Kuwait. Oil prices again soared briefly, from about $18 to almost $40 per barrel, but stabilized in the range of $20 per barrel as a coalition opposed to Iraqi occupation of Kuwait took shape. After the expulsion of Iraqi troops from Kuwait, they quickly fell again. Saudi revenues soared during the brief price spike. The kingdom expanded production in part to keep prices stable but mostly to recover market share lost during the 1980s.

The costs incurred by the Saudis in the Kuwait conflict were even greater than their revenues. Saudi oil export revenues in 1990–91 averaged $41.5 billion annually compared to $24 billion in 1989. The combined hard currency and budgetary costs of the conflict were about $60 billion, however, forcing the government to take the politically painful step of increasing foreign borrowing for the short fall.[14] (The kingdom had begun foreign borrowing in the late 1980s.)

In the early 1990s, another political factor arose that could have a future destabilizing effect on the oil market—a movement among the major consuming countries to levy additional energy taxes. Energy taxes are not new, but Saudi Arabia and other producing countries have become increasingly concerned that a new wave of proposed taxes is designed primarily to transfer revenues from them to the consumer states. For example, the European Community earned about $200 billion in taxes on about 10.3 mbd of petroleum products in 1991 compared to exporters' revenues of only $64 billion.[15]

One of the main arguments used to justify an energy tax, both in Europe and the United States, has been to clean up and protect the environment. The Saudis, however, are not convinced that environmental protection is the real issue. They see a decided bias against oil even though other fuels, such as coal, are even more polluting. More important, they believe the driving force behind the new taxes is the need for revenues. This was particularly the case in the United States in 1993 when the Clinton administration included an energy tax as a part of its economic policy. In the Saudi view, the administration seemed more interested in lowering the U.S. deficit than in cleaning up the environment.

Despite strong anxiety about new energy taxes in Europe and the United States, the Saudis have maintained a policy of caution in confronting the issue, apparently recognizing that strong measures such as running up the price of oil through production cuts to close the gap between the prices of taxed and untaxed oil are unrealistic so long as the glut continues.

LOOKING AHEAD: SHORT-TERM REVENUE NEEDS AND LONG-TERM OIL POLICY

When revenues declined drastically during the 1980s, Saudi Arabia resorted to a few fiscal restraints but avoided really painful austerity measures, gambling that the glut would end before the kingdom exhausted the huge reserves it had amassed in the 1970s. To an extent, it lost the gamble. By the end of the Kuwait conflict, the kingdom was no longer a cash-rich country. Since then, its short- and medium-term needs for revenues have again begun to affect its oil policies.

Having taken the brunt of OPEC production and revenue cuts in the 1980s, the Saudis had totally abandoned their desire to be the swing producer by the early 1990s, stating that they intended to produce more than 8 mbd and that if the glut persisted they would not reduce production under 7 mbd to stabilize prices. They claimed that the market should determine prices, not artificial shifts in production rates (the essence of their swing producer policy).

The competition between long-term Saudi maximization of oil revenues through moderate prices and secure supply and meeting the kingdom's short-term revenue needs through higher prices is likely to continue until there is again a tight world oil market and revenues increase. Nevertheless, without another political disruption of the market, this might not happen for several years, perhaps not until after the turn of the century.

In the meantime, it will be interesting to track government-industry relations. Saudi Aramco, despite being a government-owned company, has continued to operate to a great extent as if it were still a commercial oil company, making planning decisions on the basis of return on investment rather than pure political expediency. This is apparent in its long-range development plans. In December 1994, it completed a program to increase productive capacity to more than 10 mbd; and despite the country's short-term cash flow problems, it is continuing its ambitious plans to develop domestic fields and also to expand its operations downstream to include refining and marketing. The first downstream acquisition was the purchase of one-half of Texaco's refining and marketing operations in the eastern and southern United States in 1988. It is also working toward refining at least half its crude oil production by the end of the decade, either at home or at refineries abroad in which the country has an equity.

Table 2. Crude Oil Production, 1990–1993 (in millions of barrels per day)

	1990	1991	1992	1993
OPEC Crude	22.7	22.7	24.0	24.7
Saudi Arabia	6.5	8.2	8.4	8.1
Kuwait	1.3	0.2	1.0	1.9
United Arab Emirates	2.0	2.3	2.3	2.2
Qatar	0.4	0.4	0.4	0.4
Iran	3.1	3.3	3.4	3.6
Iraq	1.9	0.2	0.4	0.6
Algeria	0.8	0.8	0.8	0.8
Nigeria	1.8	1.9	1.9	1.9
Libya	1.4	1.5	1.4	1.4
Gabon	0.3	0.3	0.3	0.3
Indonesia	1.2	1.4	1.4	1.3
Venezuela	2.2	2.3	2.2	2.3
Non-OPEC (Crude and cond.)	40.9	40.4	39.6	38.9
United States	9.0	7.4	7.2	6.9
FSU	11.5	10.4	9.0	7.8
North Sea	3.9	3.8	4.2	4.5
Other	16.5	18.9	19.2	19.7
OPEC Cond./NGL	2.1	2.1	2.1	2.2
Processing gains	1.4	1.4	1.4	1.5
Total Production	67.0	66.6	67.1	67.3

Source: Petroleum Finance Company, Washington, D.C.

All these plans will cost billions of dollars in investment capital and already have been tempered by the need to divert funds from development to more pressing short-term government revenue needs. In this environment, the wonder is not that the government has squeezed Saudi Aramco for revenues but that it has not done so even more, particularly when compared to other government-owned oil companies. Part of the answer might be the legacy of years in dealing with former American owners. A greater motivating factor, however, appears to be the government's desire to be seen internationally as not only a price moderate but also a responsible, dependable oil supplier. Such a reputation is enhanced by allowing Saudi Aramco to act at least to a degree as a commercial oil company. When the chips are down, however, there is little doubt that politics will drive oil policy, at least in the short run.

5

Economic Development and Modernization

Like all facets of life in Saudi Arabia, the economic system is inexorably linked to Islam. One of the most formal Islamic restrictions on economic activity is *riba* (interest on a capital loan), which is considered usury and is banned by Islamic law. The Saudi banking system has found ways to circumvent this restriction, however, such as charging fees rather than interest for loans. There are other specific Islamic legal restrictions, but they have not greatly inhibited modern banking or economic development. Probably the greatest Islamic influence on the economic system is Saudi Arabia's Islamic culture rather than Islamic law.

Saudi Islamic Capitalism

The Hanbali school of Islamic jurisprudence that guides Saudi Arabia's ultra-conservative Islamic approach to social and legal matters is, ironically, one of the most liberal on economic and commercial matters. It is no accident, therefore, that the kingdom's economy is one of the most wide open in the world, and that Saudi business practices are among the most free-wheeling.

Two behavioral factors also affect Saudi economic activity. The first involves attitudes toward work and wealth. As products of an Islamic society, Saudis have attitudes toward wealth that are substantially different from those in the West. Islam does not distinguish between the world of the flesh and the world of the spirit; both are within the dominion of God's creation, and no guilt is attached to amassing private wealth. God has bountifully blessed Saudi Arabia, and there is no stigma attached to each Saudi's obtaining as much of that bounty as possible. (The Islamic world sanctioned women's owning and inheriting property long before the West did, and Saudi women number among the kingdom's wealthiest persons.)

On the other hand, Islam teaches that as God provides wealth to the rich, it is incumbent on them to see to the needs of the less fortunate, not merely as an act of generosity but as a religious obligation, *Zakat*. Conversely, it is the right of the poor to have their needs met. Because most of the wealth of the kingdom accrues to the public sector, the government has become the principal source of public welfare programs, not in emulation of Western social welfare doctrines but as a civic and religious obligation. Private citizens are not relieved of their obligation, however, and the traditional system of private religious endowments for the poor (awqaf) is administered through the Ministry of Awqaf.

Of even more significance than attitudes toward wealth are attitudes toward work. With the emphasis on enjoying God's bounty, Saudi Arabia has never developed a strong work ethic. Although Saudis had to work hard simply to survive during the poverty-stricken days before the discovery of oil, they did not develop the sense that hard work was a form of seeking God's grace or that work simply for its own sake was morally uplifting. Herein lies one of the greatest challenges for the economic future of the country: unless the society develops a stronger work ethic, no amount of social welfare programs can prepare Saudi society to be fully self-reliant economically and not dependent on foreign labor in key sectors of the economy.

The second factor that shapes Saudi economic activity is the dominance of the public sector over the private sector. Saudi Arabia is a classic example of the rentier state. In contrast to the West, where the government collects tax revenues in order to provide public services to the citizens, the main task of the Saudi government is to distribute state-accrued oil revenues in the form of goods, services, and subsidies to the people in the most equitable way. Equitable distribution of wealth is a far more difficult task than it might seem at first glance, with social and political implications that directly affect the stability of the kingdom. Moreover, to the degree that it creates public economic dependence on the government—a classic symptom of the rentier state—and saps the private sector of initiative and industriousness, it may end up as a very mixed blessing indeed.

A third factor shaping Saudi economic activity is the Saudi business ethic. There is a widespread perception in the West that Saudi business and government practices are riddled with corruption and that such practices are evidence of moral decay that will inevitably lead to political instability and collapse. One of the primary difficulties in understanding Saudi corruption is the great difference between Saudi and Western business ethics. If one accepts the definition of corruption as a deviation from an accepted norm, one must begin with Saudi standards of business ethics. In addition to Islamic injunctions, a number of unwritten rules regulate Saudi business practices in both the public and the private sectors. Generally, it is the unwitting Western businessman most disadvantaged by these practices who cries corruption.

The first rule is that all government and private business practices are highly personalized and conducted on the basis of mutual trust. Without that trust, a contracting firm is likely to encounter all sorts of petty irritants undermining the profitability of the contract. Second, the party expressing the greater desire to conclude a contract is inevitably at a disadvantage, an expression of an age-old Middle Eastern principle of supply and demand. Third, and perhaps most important, caveat emptor is the governing principle of business negotiations. For goods and services one charges what the market will bear, and let the buyer beware. As a result, one must be fully aware of the market value before attempting a transaction. Finally, it is not necessarily morally reprehensible to accept payment for services rendered that would be considered a conflict of interest or even graft in the West. At the same time, no payment is due if no service is rendered, although that does not prevent some people from seeking unearned payments.

These rules are easily recognizable to anyone who has frequented the suqs and bazaars of the Middle East. It is only when millions of dollars are involved that the practices have been condemned as morally corrupt. As Western businessmen have learned the rules of doing business in Saudi Arabia since the mad rush for petrodollars in the 1970s, charges of corruption have declined. Moreover, the development of more efficient accounting practices in both public and private sectors and the cash flow problems of the government requiring more stringent oversight of public expenditures have also lessened the most egregious examples of such practices. Given the high level of personal trust that pervades Saudi business practices, however, it is doubtful that Saudi businessmen and government contractors will ever emulate the litigious practices of the West.

Ironically, there is a certain egalitarian quality to Saudi government contracting practices, creating the opportunity for all income groups, not merely those at the top, to participate in the transfer of public funds to the private sector. Although Western critics have focused on members of the royal family involved in such practices, the same rules are practiced at all levels of society. It would be immensely destabilizing if such practices were halted at the bottom while the most influential levels, particularly the royal family, were still able to use their influence for financial advantage.

There is another way in which these practices actually enhance stability. Much of the under-the-table moneys accruing to senior Saudi political leaders are not for private gain but go to ensure that government and military personnel have a stake in the regime and the motivation to remain in public service rather than take more lucrative jobs in the private sector. Conceptually, these "extrabudgetary transactions" are more in the nature of maintaining high overhead costs to co-opt potential dissidents and retain badly needed expertise in government than of corruption in the Western sense of the term—though the two are certainly not mutually exclusive.

In the long run, such practices must be curtailed to avoid political friction among a growing class of technocrats who demand that government and business advancement must be based on merit. The transition must be a careful one, however, to avoid the disruptions of practices that are as old as the Middle East.

THE PRE-OIL ECONOMY

In order to see how the Saudi economy has reached its present state, it would be helpful to trace its historic origins. In the nineteenth century, Najd, the Saudi heartland, was one of the poorest countries on earth. The economy was based on nomadic animal husbandry and subsistence farming in the oasis towns and villages. To the east, in al-Hasa and al-Qatif oases, relatively large-scale irrigated farming took place; and on the Gulf coast, fishing, pearl diving, and maritime commerce on ocean-going dhows were the main means of livelihood.

The Hijaz had a far more sophisticated economy based on the Hajj trade (see chapter 6). Virtually everyone in the Hijaz benefited in one way or another from the yearly influx of pilgrims to Makkah and al-Madinah. Hajj fees represented the major source of government income. In the private sector, the Hajj brought commercial opportunities for the sale and resale of goods and services. Most of the great Hijazi merchant families, who for years formed the backbone of the Saudi commercial establishment, got their start in the Hajj trade.

Those whose livelihoods were most directly linked to the Hajj comprised the Hajj service industry. Organized centuries ago into guilds that were similar to the medieval guilds of Europe, their general makeup has not changed greatly to this day. They consist of *mutawwifs,* who serve as guides for the holy rites in Makkah and environs; *Zamzamis,* whose name came from their original function of providing Hajjis with water from the holy well of Zamzam in the Haram Mosque in Makkah and who now assist mutawwifs in guiding Hajjis; *wakils* (literally "deputies" of the mutawwifs), who meet and process Hajjis in Jiddah; and *dalils,* who serve as guides in al-Madinah. There were others in past times, including *sambukjis,* who rowed Hajjis ashore in small boats called sambuks from ships anchored in the outer harbors of the ports of Jiddah and Yanbu' before there were adequate landing facilities.

Of even greater economic importance was the retail and entrepôt trade associated with the Hajj. Until the mid-twentieth century, Hajjis stayed longer periods, sometimes years, before returning home; and the bulk of retail commerce in the Hijaz occurred during the Hajj season. Although oil revenues long ago replaced Hajj revenues as the backbone of the Saudi economy, the Hajj season still remains a major retail commercial season.

Even the nomadic tribes of the Hijaz and western Najd benefited from the Hajj, charging overland Hajjis traveling through their tribal areas for "protection." Indeed, under the Ottomans and the post-World War I Hijazi government, the Hajj served as a great opportunity for Hijazis and Najdi tribes alike to shake down unsuspecting pilgrims for as much money as possible.

When Abd al-Aziz Al Saud took over the Hijaz in 1924–25, the Hajj trade became the main source of revenue for the entire country. As king, he went to great lengths to correct the irregularities attached to the Hajj trade; but he was still heavily dependent on the Hajj revenues as the principal source of public and private revenue, both from fees paid by the Hajjis and retail commerce during the Hajj season. In the 1930s the combination of the Great Depression and the political upheavals leading to World War II drastically reduced the numbers of those making the Hajj, and Saudi revenues declined at an alarming rate. By the outbreak of World War II, the kingdom was on the verge of economic collapse. As we saw in chapter 4, first the oil companies and then the United States through Lend-Lease aid kept the kingdom economically solvent.

FROM SUBSISTENCE TO AFFLUENCE

After World War II, oil revenues finally began to accrue in sufficient quantities to enable Saudi Arabia to cease living off foreign handouts for its economic survival. Even so, the transformation from a bare subsistence level in the interior and traditional merchandizing in the Hijaz to a major oil economy did not occur overnight.

Before the war, both public and private financial institutions were rudimentary at best. Although the Saudi Ministry of Finance had been created in 1933, economic policy decisions were made according to the highly personalized traditional system that had been in existence in the Arabian peninsula for centuries. Paper money was distrusted and none was in circulation. Financial transactions, including Aramco royalty payments, were made in specie, generally Saudi silver riyals and British gold sovereigns, although the Bedouins often preferred Austrian Maria Theresa silver talers.

Private sector banking was still carried on primarily through traditional money changers and branches of foreign banks, the earliest of which had been established to service Hajjis from their colonial territories. Even after the opening of modern banks, many locals continued to patronize the money changers in their picturesque stalls in the suqs. Dealing in incredibly large sums, these traditional bankers stayed abreast of the latest currency quotations worldwide and themselves kept accounts in the modern banks.

The first foreign banking operations were maintained by a British trading firm, Gelatly Hanky and Company, which established a Jiddah branch in 1884.

In 1955, it transferred its accounts to the British Bank of the Middle East, which had opened a branch in Jiddah in 1950. The first foreign bank operating in the kingdom was the Netherlands Trading Society, established in 1926 to deal with Dutch East Indian (Indonesian) Hajjis. The Dutch Bank, as it was known, initially conducted most of the international monetary transactions for the kingdom. The oldest (and largest) Saudi domestic bank, the National Commercial Bank, was registered in 1953 by two prominent money changers, Abd al-Aziz al-Ka'ki and Salim ibn Mahfouz.[1]

In the years immediately following the war, both Saudis and Westerners called for reforming the kingdom's finances. The task was formidable. Public attitudes failed to distinguish between public and private revenues, believing that what God had bountifully bestowed on the country was there for the taking by any Saudi who could lay claim to it. Few Saudis were technically qualified to understand the complexities of government finance, including the aging King Abd al-Aziz and his finance minister, Abdallah Sulayman. Not only were public attitudes a hindrance to reform, but Islamic tradition, with its proscription on interest payments as usury, presented additional problems. Public distrust of paper money and banking in general stemmed from the association of both with usurious practices.

The influx of oil revenues—from almost nothing in 1945 to $57 million in 1950 and $340.8 million in 1955—required a vastly improved system for managing government monetary and fiscal affairs. Moreover, many foreign banks had established branches in the kingdom after the war, creating a need for more comprehensive banking regulations. Although the British and French made a number of recommendations for reforms, the Americans were most involved in the early phases of creating modern Saudi monetary and fiscal institutions. With government finances in chaos, the U.S. Export-Import Bank loaned the kingdom $10 million in 1946 and another $15 million in 1950 to keep the government solvent. During the same period, partly in response to Saudi requests and partly on its own initiative, the United States began offering technical assistance.

In 1948, George Eddy, a gold expert with the Office of International Finance in the U.S. Treasury Department, and Raymond F. Mikesell from the State Department traveled to the kingdom to study currency reform. Saudi Arabia was then on a double standard (gold and silver), and market fluctuations between the two made maintaining a stable currency virtually impossible. The Eddy-Mikesell mission made recommendations but little headway. In August 1950, another U.S. mission, headed by John F. Greaney, arrived to help design an income tax (since abolished).

It was not until 1951 that major reforms got under way. In January, Saudi Arabia signed a Point Four technical assistance agreement with the United

States that was to have a major impact on monetary and fiscal reforms. The following summer, a Point Four financial mission under Arthur N. Young arrived to help reform the budgetary and administrative system of the Ministry of Finance and improve the tariff system.[2]

It was in monetary reform that the Young mission made its largest impact—by recommending the creation of a central bank. On April 20, 1952, the Saudi Arabian Monetary Agency (SAMA) was created. The term *monetary agency* was chosen in order to avoid mention of a bank or a financial institution; the Saudis feared that the latter could connote charging or paying interest, which is proscribed by Islam and were specifically forbidden in the charter.

SAMA's initial charter listed as its objectives: (a) to strengthen the currency of Saudi Arabia, to stabilize it in relation to foreign currencies, and to avoid the losses resulting to the government and people from fluctuations in the exchange value of Saudi Arabian coins whose rates have not so far been fixed in relation to foreign currencies which form the major part of the government's reserve; and (b) to aid the Ministry of Finance in centralizing the receipts and expenditures of the government in accordance with authorized budget and in controlling payments so that all branches of the government shall abide by the government.[3] In addition to these responsibilities, the charter also tasked SAMA with regulating the commercial banks and managing the kingdom's reserves. The first two governors of SAMA were Americans, the third a Pakistani. Thereafter, Saudis have managed what has become one of the most powerful central banking institutions in the world.

SAMA officially opened on October 4, 1952, and immediately embarked on currency reform. One of the first measures was to issue Saudi gold sovereigns, making the kingdom the only country at the time with a fiduciary gold coin. Silver riyals were then pegged to the sovereigns at a ratio of forty riyals to one sovereign. (The sovereigns were withdrawn in 1954 because of a flood of solid gold "counterfeit" sovereigns from abroad, taking advantage of the higher price of the sovereign than its bullion equivalent.)

Even more creative was SAMA's introduction of paper currency. SAMA's original charter prohibited it from issuing paper currency due to local resistance and concern that it might encourage anti-Islamic banking practices. As a result, large transactions became burdensome. For example, with only one denomination of silver coin available to meet the monthly payroll, Aramco had to purchase, transport, and store sixty tons of silver each month.[4]

Hajjis also had difficulty exchanging their foreign currencies for riyals and carrying around the heavy silver coins. In July 1953, SAMA began issuing scrip which it called "Hajj receipts" in denominations of one, five, and ten riyals. Hajjis could exchange their currencies for the Hajj receipts redeemable at any bank for riyals, which greatly facilitated foreign currency transactions during the Hajj season. More important, because the scrip was not issued as legal tender and was fully backed by silver and gold, there was no local resistance to it, and it soon began to circulate throughout the country. By August 7, during the 1953 Hajj season, SR (Saudi riyals) 23 million worth of Hajj receipts had been issued; by September 10, at the end of the season, only 30 percent of it had been redeemed. By 1955, when a rise in the price of silver resulted in Saudi riyals' being smuggled out of the country, the Hajj receipts had become accepted as de facto currency throughout the kingdom. Beginning in June 1961, after SAMA's charter had been changed, it issued the first paper currency in denominations of one, five, ten, fifty, and one hundred riyals. In 1964, the Hajj receipts were withdrawn from circulation.

Paradoxically, during the mid to late 1950s, when the basic government infrastructure for managing the national economy was being established, the economy itself was in shambles. King Saud ibn Abd al-Aziz, who succeeded his father in 1953, was simply not up to the task of overseeing the growing oil wealth. In 1958, he was forced to name his brother and heir apparent, Prince Faysal ibn Abd al-Aziz, as prime minister. Faysal quickly set out to bring order to the economy. Among other things, he secured the appointment of Anwar Ali, a Pakistani, as governor of SAMA for six months, on secondment from the International Monetary Fund (that is, he was technically still an employee of the IMF, with full reemployment rights, but paid by the Saudi government). Through Faysal's efforts, Ali remained in the position for sixteen years until his death in 1974, the longest secondment in the history of the IMF.

Under Anwar Ali and his Saudi successors, SAMA developed into a leading financial institution. In the 1970s, for example, it was prepared to deal with the myriad of problems associated with the dramatic rise in oil revenues, which could have otherwise created a chaotic monetary and banking environment. In addition to other tasks, Ali and his successor, Abd al-Aziz al-Qurayshi, oversaw the Saudization of foreign banks, transferring a majority interest to local investors. Thus, the First National City Bank's Saudi operation became the Saudi-American Bank; the British Bank of the Middle East became the Saudi-British Bank; and so on. Characteristic of Anwar Ali, he began with the Saudization of the National Bank of Pakistan (now the Al-Jazirah Bank).

SAMA was also instrumental in the creation of specialized government-owned development banks, including the Saudi Arabian Agricultural Bank, the Saudi Industrial Development Fund, and the Saudi Credit Bank (all of which give concessionary financing to Saudi nationals) and the Saudi International Bank, set up in London in 1975 to train Saudi nationals in international banking.

King Saud balked at becoming a figurehead, and in 1960 he again took the reins of power. After two years characterized by mismanagement and intrigue, he was compelled a second time to relinquish power and in 1964 was forced to abdicate in favor of Faysal.

FROM OIL STATE TO OIL GIANT

King Faysal, like his father before him, was a man of extraordinary vision. The princes and commoners he chose to hold senior government positions have never been analyzed collectively, but they were a remarkable group. Many are still in office or just retiring, and their places are being filled by younger men who were for many years under their tutelage.

Faysal's vision of economic and social development still guides the country's basic policy in those spheres. Heavily influenced by his mother's family, the Al al-Shaykhs, he placed Islam at the center of his development philosophy, which could be summed up in a single phrase: "modernization without secularization." Essentially, Faysal wanted to preserve the pre-industrial, Islamic social system molded by his Al Saud and Al al-Shaykh forebears while seeking to offer his people the fruits of the industrial age that oil revenues put within their grasp.

Because modernization and secularization tend to go hand in hand, creating a development strategy to accomplish this goal was a difficult task. It was a mark of his political skills as well as his foresight that King Faysal succeeded so well, gently pushing his people toward modernization but no farther or faster than they could tolerate. For example, to meet the criticism of religious leaders that the radio was an instrument of Satan, Faysal ensured that prime broadcast time on newly established Saudi radio was dedicated to reading the Quran and other religious topics.

In contrast to the evolution of political institutions, Saudi economic development was the result of a formal planning process. In 1968, the deputy petroleum minister, Hisham Nazir, was made head of the Central Planning Organization (CPO), a dubious promotion because the CPO was then a fairly moribund institution. Nazir, by force of personality and drive, reinvigorated it, making it the principal planning vehicle in the Saudi government.

This was a considerable accomplishment given the fact that the various ministries all jealously guarded their bureaucratic turf—a severe threat to central planning, which requires interagency cooperation. Nazir's former boss, petroleum minister Yamani, was a particular rival, though they were personal friends. In recognition of Nazir's success and the rising importance of central planning, the CPO was raised to a ministry in 1975.

The central planning process that the CPO and later the Planning Ministry created bore no resemblance to the development planning process in the former Soviet Union or Communist Eastern Europe. Saudi five-year plans can better be described as a combination of wish lists and statements of intent. They are not intended as detailed instructions for budgetary expenditures, nor should they be considered outside the context of the flexible Middle Eastern sense of time. Budget allocations and target dates should be viewed impressionistically rather than literally. The plans, however, are fairly accurate indicators of the direction the Saudis believed they should be taking at the time and what lessons they had learned from the previous plan.

The CPO, working closely with the Stanford Research Institute, instituted the first Saudi five-year development plan in 1970. With a relatively modest initial budget of $9.2 billion, it contained three primary goals, all closely aligned to the development philosophy of King Faysal: first, to preserve the basic Islamic religious and social values of the country; second, to increase Saudi military defense capability; and third, to prepare the country for diversification in the post-oil era.[5]

Although no one knew it at the time, the first plan would overlap with the enormous rise in oil revenues beginning with the energy crisis of 1973. As a result, the economy expanded at a dizzying pace (the GDP increased 112 percent between 1970 and 1975) and would have done so whether or not there had been a plan.

The second five-year plan (1975–80), with a proposed budget of $149 billion, made the first plan seem minuscule in comparison. Continuing along the same lines, it emphasized social and economic infrastructure and building up the agricultural and industrial sectors, particularly petrochemicals. The Saudis also embarked on building two major industrial centers, Yanbuʿ on the Red Sea and Jubayl on the Gulf—among the most ambitious development projects ever attempted. The cities were originally designed to house a range of refining and petrochemical manufacturing operations plus a steel manufacturing operation fired in large part by excess Saudi natural gas. The concessionary cost of gas helped the projects to succeed but lowered Saudi Aramco's commitment to expanding domestic gas production, which may in the long run dampen further expansion. In the meantime, industrial development at the two cities has attracted additional enterprises, both public and private, including fabrication and processing plants for both local markets and re-export.

The second plan placed special emphasis on social welfare and development projects, including free medical service, subsidized housing, and free education. The Saudi educational system was greatly expanded, and thousands of young Saudis were sent abroad for further study until national universities could absorb them. This emphasis on public education still continues. From a mere 33,000 in 1953, the Saudi student population rose to 2.65 million by 1989, of which some 1.16 million were girls; and it continues to expand. Part of the cost of such rapid expansion is a lowering of standards, but this does not negate a tremendous achievement for a country that was 95 percent illiterate at the end of World War II. A university system was also created that includes the King Fahd University of Petroleum and Minerals, founded by Aramco in 1963 in Dhahran; King Saud University in Riyadh, formerly Riyadh University; King Abd al-Aziz University in Jiddah with campuses in al-Madinah and Abha, originally founded as a private institution in 1967 and changed to a state university in 1971; and King Faysal University with campuses in Hufuf and Dammam. There is also a more traditional Islamic university system, including Imam Muhammad ibn Saud Islamic University in Riyadh, the University of al-Madinah, and Umm al-Qura University in Makkah. Their main function is to train Islamic judges, teachers, and scholars for government ministries and agencies where such background is required, such as the ministries of Justice and Education, and the "morality police" (committees for encouraging virtue and preventing vice).

The second five-year plan coincided with the oil boom years of the 1970s and thus faced no financial constraints. By the end of the period, the lesson that foreign-aid donors had learned in other developing countries had became obvious to the Saudis as well—that there are limits to how much capital expenditure an economy can absorb, particularly in the absence of an adequate pool of technical expertise, a bureaucratic tradition, and a well-ingrained work ethic. With a low absorptive capacity for capital expenditure, massive spending created inflation, waste, and graft on a grand scale.

Nevertheless, the Saudis succeeded in putting into place much of the basic economic and social infrastructure needed for a modern economy; created a viable non-oil industrial sector, particularly in import substitution items; and transformed the Saudi population into one of the most highly educated in the region. Moreover, they still spent considerably less than they earned in the 1970s, amassing foreign-exchange holdings of about $150 billion.

The Oil Glut: Living in Reduced Circumstances

When the third five-year plan (1980–85) was approved by the Council of Ministers in May 1980, no one yet knew that the oil boom was about to end and a period of extended glut about to begin. The third plan had an approved budget of $250 billion, reflecting projected oil revenues that were wholly unrealistic in light of the greatly reduced oil prices that have persisted since that time. It was eventually scaled back to about $180 billion.

Nevertheless, the planners did have a good grasp of the state of Saudi economic development. The third plan emphasized consolidating previous economic gains and reducing inflation, a major problem during the second plan. Due to the drastic reduction in revenues in the 1980s, the problem of inflation solved itself. The plan also emphasized social and physical infrastructure

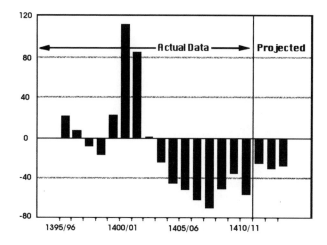

Figure 18. Saudi budget deficits and surpluses, 1395/96–1413/14 (c. 1975–93). *Source:*
David Rehfuss, Riyad Bank.

completion and Saudization, particularly in reducing dependence on foreign
labor.

When the oil glut began in the early 1980s and oil prices started their long
decline, the Saudis made a calculated decision to maintain economic and social
development and military spending levels by drawing down foreign-exchange
reserves. They counted on rising prices eventually to put an end to deficit
financing.

No one foresaw that the glut would last so long or that the Saudi role as
swing producer would force it to cut production drastically to maintain price
stability. From 1981 to 1985, production dropped from 9.8 mbd to 2.34 mbd,
and oil revenues made up less than half of budgetary expenditures. In addition, no one foresaw that not even a fraction of the billions of dollars loaned to
shore up Iraq in the Iran-Iraq war would ever be repaid or that Iraq would
turn on its former benefactors by invading Kuwait and precipitating the Gulf
War, which cost the Saudis another $55 billion. In addition, the continuing
postwar military threats from Iran and Iraq prompted a higher level of Saudi
defense spending.

By 1994, as a net result of more than a decade of deficit financing, Saudi
Arabia had drawn a large part of its foreign-exchange holdings and was expe-
riencing increasingly serious structural budgetary and current account deficits. In 1995, the government finally began to take remedial action. One of the
indicators of official concern are the recent Saudi five-year plans. The fourth
plan (1985–90) was scaled down in size to under $140 billion and emphasized

Table 3. Saudi Non-Oil GDP by Major Economic Activity (as constant 1970 prices in billions of riyals)

	1986	1987	1988	1989	1990	1991	1992
Transport, storage, and communications	4.4	4.3	4.3	4.3	4.5	4.5	4.5
Manufacturing and refining	5.4	6.1	6.7	6.5	7.5	8.4	8.8
Agriculture, forestry, and fisheries	3.6	4.2	4.7	5.0	5.2	5.3	5.4
Electricity, gas, and water	1.0	1.0	1.1	1.2	1.2	1.3	1.3
Construction	3.7	3.6	3.4	3.4	3.4	3.5	3.6
Trade, hotels, and restaurants	8.0	7.9	7.8	7.8	7.9	8.0	8.1
Petroleum and natural gas	11.1	9.5	11.6	11.6	14.5	17.7	18.6

Source: David Rehfuss, Riyad Bank.

economic efficiency and productivity as well as the importance of a strong private sector. The fifth plan (1990–95) was reduced even more, to just over $100 billion. Following the general lines of previous plans, it sets modest targets for expansion of social services and economic infrastructure and continued support for non-oil sectors of the economy.

The sixth plan (1995–2000) is also expected to be scaled down. It continues to emphasize strengthening the private sector, including more privatization. The other major goals of the plan, announced in mid-1993, are better rationalization of government expenditures (apparently reflecting awareness of the need for more strategic planning), manpower training, and Saudization.

Most of Saudi debt is internal (payable in riyals), amounting to about 50 percent of the GDP in 1992, but this compares favorably with U.S. internal debt, which amounted to about 66 percent in 1992. More important, the well-managed Saudi debt management program, which sells bonds on the domestic bond market, combined with an abundance of highly liquid private sector and institutional money and a lack of alternative attractive domestic instruments to absorb it, ensures that the kingdom will continue to be able to pay its obligations despite its cash flow problems.

THE SAUDI PRIVATE SECTOR

The predominance of the government-owned oil sector has often caused the Saudi private sector to be overlooked. The private sector entered a period of rapid growth following the Kuwait war, albeit with generous subsidies from

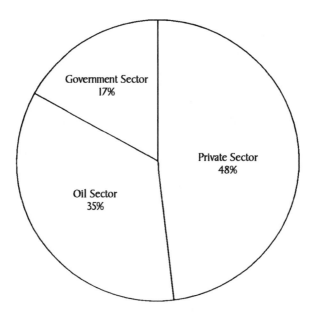

Figure 19. Saudi GDP by major sector, 1995. *Source:* David Rehfuss, Riyad Bank.

the government. Although the initial boom appeared to be over by mid-decade, many Saudi businessmen believe that the private sector is still basically sound and is likely to gain a momentum all its own in the coming years, significantly lessening Saudi dependence on the oil-dominated public sector.

After a recession in the mid-1980s, private capital began flowing back into the kingdom. The favorable outcome of Desert Storm, in particular, triggered a major repatriation of capital. Annual private capital inflows increased from $8.2 billion in 1989 to $14.1 billion in 1991 and were still at $12.7 billion in 1992. Repatriation of capital reflected increased confidence in not only national security but also growing commercial opportunities that were formerly lacking. Declining public sector transfers to the private sector in the 1980s and 1990s actually strengthened the private sector, encouraging a new class of young, Western-educated Saudi entrepreneurs seeking investment opportunities for their own capital, not just lucrative government contracts. This could be one of the most significant and positive developments in the Saudi economy in years.

In 1992, the private sector comprised about 35 percent of the GDP, with the government sector making up 28 percent and the oil sector the remaining 37 percent. Non-oil industry is a mix of public and private enterprise and includes more than 2,000 factories employing about 175,000 workers, most of them non-Saudis.

Table 4. Saudi Agricultural Production, 1988–1992 (in thousands of tons)

	1988	1989	1990	1991 (est.)	1992 (est.)	1990/91 (%)
Wheat	3,267	3,285	3,463	3,861–4,000	· 4,100	2.5–6
Barley	285	331	362	500	—	38
Dates	640	518	519	545	—	5

Source: David Rehfuss, Riyad Bank.

Private agriculture has been the fastest growing sector of the economy, increasing to about 7.5 of the total GDP by 1992. Saudi development plans have nearly all stressed agricultural development as a means of economic diversification, self-sufficiency in food production, and improving the standard of living in rural areas and retarding urbanization. The greatest recipients of government agricultural subsidies have not been small farmers but large-scale operations, particularly grain producers in Qasim, that use modern irrigation from underground aquifers and employ an almost totally non-Saudi work force. The kingdom is largely self-sufficient in foodstuffs and now exports wheat, dates, dairy products, eggs, fish, poultry, and vegetables. It has also created a strong agribusiness, including food processing and packaging plants, and a service industry, selling irrigation pumps and pipes, fertilizers and farm equipment. Lower government subsidies for wheat and barley, however, announced in 1993, will probably slow substantially the rate of expansion of the agricultural sector.

In addition to private investors, private commercial banks are becoming increasingly important as a source of capital. As I have noted, the Saudi private banking system has taken longer to mature than those of other Gulf countries, mainly because of the Islamic proscription on interest. In the last few years, however, it has come into its own. Funding capital expenditures in the oil sector is a good example. Although capital expenditures for oil production facilities will continue to come mainly from government companies (such as Saudi Aramco) and government funding, 25 to 30 percent of the capital requirements for downstream operations is expected to come from private commercial banks over the next decade and another 20 percent from private Saudi and international investors.

THE IMPACT OF ECONOMICS ON POLITICS

Much external concern has been expressed about the linkage between Saudi deficit spending and political instability. There is certainly a link between economics and politics, evidenced by the collapse of the Soviet Union, but Saudi political stability is not solely dependent on government welfare. The kingdom will never be so dependent as the West on a social security system so long as Saudi extended families assume their traditional responsibility of ensuring the economic well-being of their members. Economic austerity policies to curb deficit spending would be no more popular in Saudi Arabia than anywhere else, but economic welfare is simply not an appropriate scale for measuring Saudi political stability given the strength and stability of family-oriented Saudi society.

This does not mean that the problems confronting the Saudi economy could not have a significant negative impact on the society, including the negative cash flow problem. External political events could also adversely affect the economy. For example, Saudi oil revenues would be drastically threatened if Saudi oil installations were hit in another Gulf war. Lifting United Nations sanctions on Iraqi oil exports, which will eventually occur, is also expected to affect Saudi oil revenues adversely by temporarily depressing world oil prices.

Demographics present another problem. With both government and social encouragement of large families and with available modern health care, annual Saudi population growth is about 3.7 percent. At that rate, demands for social and physical infrastructure will continue to grow, placing added strains on the budget. Moreover, with the number of college graduates increasing by 10 to 15 percent in recent years, the economy's ability to absorb them is also strained.

Government concern about this development was a major factor in pushing Saudization of the labor force. While Saudization has increased Saudi equity in formerly foreign companies, it has not reduced dependence on foreign labor, which is more productive than Saudi labor due in large part to negative Saudi attitudes toward certain kinds of work. Lower Saudi productivity is exacerbated by high salaries; Saudis now often command larger salaries than their foreign counterparts. All in all, Saudization is a mixed blessing because it tends to reduce Saudi Arabia's energy-based competitive advantage.

Prioritizing budget allocations is another major problem. Bearing in mind that each ministry more or less negotiates its allocations, the process can be very competitive and hectic. Big-ticket items such as additional arms purchases, expansion of the two holy mosques in Makkah and al-Madinah, and meeting foreign-aid requests can all be amply justified in terms of national security, guardianship of the two holy places, and foreign-policy prerogatives; but the government cannot meet every justifiable request and balance the budget.

Another source of deficit spending that Saudis may yet have to face is how better to regulate the modern-day version of the traditional shaykh's responsibility for the welfare of his people—the extrabudgetary subsidies by ministers and agency heads to those under them. Because these practices contribute to political stability, its curtailment must be done gradually and with care. In a time of budget deficit and the concomitant need for increased oversight of government expenditures, some way will have to be found to regularize and limit these expenditures as well as prioritizing allocations in light of competing financial requirements. The most logical approach is to introduce more strategic planning.

In sum, while economic conditions do affect political stability in Saudi Arabia, the kingdom's strong, family-based society is still strong insurance that economic downturns will not create the kind of political unrest found in many developing countries.

6

The Hajj

Pilgrimages to sacred shrines are an integral part of most of the world's great religions, including Islam. The Hajj, or Great Pilgrimage to Makkah, is one of the five pillars (basic tenets) of Islam. All adult believers who are able must perform the Hajj at least once in their lifetimes. *Sura* (Chapter) 3:90–91 of the Quran states: "The first House of Worship founded for mankind was in Bakka [Makkah]. Blessed and Guidance to mankind. In it are evident signs, even the Maqam Ibrahim [the Standing Place of Abraham]; and whoever enters is safe. And the Pilgrimage to the Temple [the Hajj] is an obligation to God from those who are able to journey there."

Each year, roughly 2.5 million of the faithful heed that injunction, creating an international religious spectacle that is virtually unique in the modern world. The Hajj rites are aired each year on Saudi television, and for even the most casual viewer it is a tremendously moving experience to watch thousands of pilgrims praying and exhorting together. For those who have saved for a lifetime and traveled from half a world away to be present at the Hajj, the experience can be the highlight of an entire life.

Many of the rites of the Hajj, and even the concept of a pilgrimage to Makkah itself, existed before the time of Muhammad. A native of Makkah, he was certainly familiar with these rites; and as he began to preach God's new revelation, Islam, he incorporated many of them into the new religion. References in the Quran link the site to Adam, who is credited with building the first Ka'ba, the dark, rectangular, stone structure that stands in the middle of the Haram Mosque. Other references link the Hajj to Ibrahim (Abraham) and Ismail (Ishmael), who are credited with building the present structure. According to legend, the Angel Jibril (Gabriel) brought to Ibrahim a stone that had stood on a nearby mountain, Jabal Abu Qubays, since the flood. This is the famous Black Stone built into the eastern corner of the Ka'ba. The stone is said to have originally been white but turned black through contact with the sins of mankind.[1] Linking the Hajj to Ibrahim and Adam, however, should not be construed as an attempt by the Prophet to increase the authenticity of the

Hajj. Seen from the Muslim perspective, the Hajj is a duty, not because of tradition but because it is the will of God.

The Hajj of A.H. 10 (A.D. 632) is called the Farewell Hajj. (The Hijriya calendar begins on July 16, 622, the beginning of the Hijra, or flight of Muhammad from Makkah to al-Madinah. The Hijriya year, designated A.H., is lunar and eleven days shorter than the Christian solar year so that the Hajj eventually falls during every season of the solar year.) Muhammad, who died in al-Madinah less than three months after the Farewell Hajj (on June 8, 632), seemed to know it was to be his last. It is therefore considered to be the culmination of his life's work. Guidance for performance of the Hajj rites comes not from the Quran but from the Prophet himself, particularly at the Farewell Hajj, and is recorded in the *Hadiths* (Traditions of the Prophet). Muhammad's observances at the Farewell Hajj are the basis for the Hajj ceremonies. At that time, he gave his final revelation, recorded in Sura 5:5: "This day, I have perfected your religion for you, completed my favor upon you, and I am well pleased that you have chosen Islam as your religion."

THE RITES OF THE HAJJ

Although the Hajj rites are based on the observances of the Prophet, particularly during the Farewell Hajj, it took two centuries for them to evolve into the definitive form observed today. There are minor technical differences between Sunnis and Shi'as and among the four Sunni schools of Islamic jurisprudence on how to perform the rites as well as how obligatory certain practices are, but in general all pilgrims observe the rites in the same manner. Moreover, because most Hajjis are anxious to observe all the rites, obligatory or not, distinctions of obligation are not very important in practice.

The Hajj rites begin with the departure from home. Those wishing to make the Hajj must have attained the age of puberty; be of sound mind; and be able politically, financially, and physically to make the trip. Before leaving, each pilgrim is enjoined to put his or her affairs in order, provide for those left behind, and make restitution for debts as well as for sins and wrongdoing. Pilgrims are also encouraged to travel with virtuous and dependable companions.

Before entering Makkah, each pilgrim must perform *Ihram*, the rite of consecration. Special stations are located outside Makkah where pilgrims traditionally perform Ihram, but in the age of modern transport the rites are now as likely to be performed on an airliner.

There are six basic acts of Ihram. The first is a formal statement of intention followed by a ritual cleansing. Where possible, this includes bathing and cutting of nails and hair. (Women usually cut three locks, whereas many men shave their heads.) Having performed this act, one may not cut one's hair or nails again or have sexual intercourse while in Ihram.

After the cleansing, the pilgrim is a *muhrim*, one who is spiritually purified, and may don special Hajj garments made of white sheeting or terry cloth. Men wear two seamless strips, one around the waist to the knees and the other around the left shoulder. Their heads must be bare. Women wear a white robe but do not cover their faces. The instep must be uncovered but sandals may be worn, and umbrellas may also be used to ward off the harsh rays of the Hijazi sun. The Hajj was designed for the worship of God, not for creature comforts.

The pilgrims then say two ritual prayers. The second, the *Talbiyya*, is repeated throughout the Hajj. It is difficult to capture the excitement and expectation of the Hajj as thousands of voices spontaneously chant the Talbiyya:

Labbayk Allahuma, labbayk!
Here am I awaiting your command, O God, Here am I!
La sharika laka, labbayk!
Thou hast no peer, here am I!
Inna al-hamda wal-ni'amata laka wal-mulk!
Yea, praise and grace art thine, and dominion!
La sharika laka, labbayk!
Thou hast no peer, here am I!

The pilgrim is now ready to enter Makkah, where two rites are performed that together constitute the 'Umra. The 'Umra may also be done without performing the Hajj rites proper, in which case it is called the Little Pilgrimage in contrast to the Hajj, or Great Pilgrimage. It does not, however, satisfy the Islamic obligation to perform the Hajj.

Two rites of the 'Umra are the *Tawaf al-Qudum* (Arrival Tawaf) and the *Sa'y*. A tawaf consists of walking seven times around the Ka'ba, considered the spiritual and geographical center of Islam. It is toward the Ka'ba that Muslims all over the world face when praying. Each year just before the Hajj it is covered with a black velvet and gold drape called the *Kiswah*.

Following the Arrival Tawaf, many pilgrims attempt to kiss the Black Stone, encased in a silver frame on the side of the Ka'ba. Due to the crowds, however, only the strongest can get near. One may also drink from the holy well of Zamzam. Legend has it that God created the well by striking a rock to provide water for Hajar (Hagar) and Ismail (Ishmael) when they were about to die of thirst as she searched for water.

Adjacent to the Haram Mosque and now a part of the mosque complex are two small hills, al-Safa and al-Marwa, about four hundred meters apart. The Sa'y consists of seven one-way trips between them to commemorate Hajar's search for water.

Figure 20. The Haram Mosque in Makkah, showing the Ka'bah. Photo by Saudi Aramco.

Up to this point, pilgrims may observe the rites at will. Some enter Ihram in advance, do the rites, and temporarily exit. To perform the Hajj rites, however, all must have performed the Arrival Tawaf and be in the state of Ihram.

The most important Hajj rites occur on the eighth through twelfth days of the Muslim month of Dhu al-Hijja. On the eighth the Ka'ba is ceremonially washed down and a special sermon delivered. The pilgrims then depart for 'Arafat, a wide, barren plain some twenty kilometers east of Makkah. Excitement begins to grow as the 2.5 million pilgrims arrive at the great tent city erected for the occasion. The preferred location is Jabal al-Rahma, the Mount of Mercy, which rises some sixty meters from the floor of the plain on the eastern side.

The climax of the Hajj occurs on the ninth day of Dhu al-Hijja, called *Yawm al-Wuquf*, or Standing Day. The wuquf lasts from noon to sunset, and each Hajji must be standing on 'Arafat at sunset or the entire Hajj is forfeited. It is a time of unmuted excitement. 'Arafat has become a huge tent city, and masses of people stretch as far as the eye can see. Everywhere is heard the chanting of the Talbiyya. In the cryptic words of tradition, the Wuquf *is* the Hajj—the supreme hours.

After sunset prayers, the wuquf is over. Then begins one of the most chaotic, stressful exercises in this or any other religious observance, the *Nafra*

Figure 21. Pilgrims at
Mina during the Hajj.
Photo by Saudi Aramco.

(literally, the "rushing;" it is also sometimes called the *Ifada*, or "pouring
forth"). Rushing hardly characterizes the surge of Hajjis from ʿArafat to
Muzdalifa, a small town about seven kilometers away. Some are on foot, and
others travel in autos and buses on the many superhighways specially built
for the occasion. It is one of the world's greatest traffic jams despite monu-
mental Saudi efforts at traffic control.

At Muzdalifa, each Hajji should say sunset and evening prayers. Special
grace can be obtained by praying at the roofless mosque called al-Mashʿar al-
Haram (the Sacred Grove). There is also another wuquf and sermon that night
at Muzdalifa. Afterward, many pilgrims hunt around in the darkness for the
seventy stones (forty-nine if the Hajj is cut short a day) to be used for the
lapidations (stone throwing) the following day.

After midnight, on the tenth of Dhu al-Hijja, everyone leaves for Mina,
another small town about eight kilometers farther east. On the far end of town
are three stone pillars, called *jamaras*, representing *shaytans*, or devils. On

that day, seven stones are thrown at the first jamara, Jamarat al-'Aqaba, but not the other two, Jamarat al-Wasta and Jamarat al-Ula. On the following three days (a pilgrim may limit it to two), seven stones each are cast at all three. After each stone, the Hajji usually recites the *Takbir: Bismillah, Allahu Akbar,* which means "In the name of God; God is most great." Those too infirm to throw the stones (or unable to push through the crowds) can delegate another to do so for them.

From the tenth to the twelfth of Dhu al-Hijja, Muslims celebrate the *'Id al-Adha,* the Feast of the Sacrifice, not only at the Hajj but throughout the Muslim world. It is a joyous celebration, characterized by visits from friends. During the 'Id, each family sacrifices an unblemished animal—generally a sheep or a goat but sometimes a camel. It is permissible to sacrifice a small fowl such as a pigeon, but most Hajjis, after going to all the expense of making the Hajj, spurn such animals. The lapidations begin the desacrilization from Ihram. For example, after stoning the first jamara, a pilgrim no longer recites the Talbiyya. Following the sacrifice, the Hajjis perform the final desacrilization rites. The first is a ceremonial haircut (cutting three hairs will do). After that, one must journey back to Makkah to complete the process. It consists primarily of the Closing Tawaf, the *Tawaf al-Ifada,* although partaking of Zamzam water and performing the Sa'y may also be done. Hajjis are then free from all Ihram restrictions and return to Mina for the rest of the 'Id al-Adha.

On the thirteenth of Dhu al-Hijja, after the final lapidations, the Hajjis prepare to leave Mina for the last time. In Makkah, they perform the *Tawaf al-Wada',* or Farewell Tawaf, after which the Hajj is officially completed and each pilgrim qualified to use the formal title "Hajj" (or "Hajji" in Farsi). Most Hajjis, however, if they have not already done so, go on to visit al-Madinah, which has thus become an integral part of the entire experience. The central attraction in al-Madinah is the Prophet's Mosque, which together with the Haram Mosque in Makkah, comprise the *Haramayn,* the two holiest shrines in Islam.

The Public Administration of the Hajj

The Hajj has had more direct influence on Saudi politics and society than virtually any other phenomenon in the country. It is, of course, the most important religious observance in the country based on numbers alone. Much of the society of the Hijaz traces its ancestry to Hajjis of bygone centuries. Economically, Hajj receipts were the backbone of the economy until the marketing of oil. Even today, it is the premier commercial season in the kingdom, similar to Christmas in Western countries.

More immediately, however, the Hajj is an exercise in public administration.[2] It is virtually impossible for anyone not experienced with the Hajj to grasp the magnitude of the administrative problems it creates. To get some idea, let us place it in a Western setting. Try to picture more than 1.8 million foreign pilgrims arriving in Norfolk, Virginia, by sea, air, and land, joined by another 600,000 to 800,000 people arriving from other parts of Virginia and neighboring states. All the non-Virginians have to be processed by health, immigration, and customs officials and sent overland to Richmond, where the observance of rites begins.

Following these rites, they must all travel about twenty kilometers out into the countryside, where they are put up in a great tent city. After sunset on a given day, they all depart, stopping to pray at a nearby village before going on to yet another tent city. After three more days, during which more than 1 million animals have been butchered, they all go back to Richmond and observe some more rites. Then most of them trek across the state to Charlottesville (the equivalent of going to al-Madinah) for a week or so before going back to Norfolk and departing for home.

But that is not all. The foreign pilgrims speak about seventy different languages, most are middle aged or older, and many are illiterate. As a comparison to the harsh Arabian climate, let us say that the Virginia Hajj occurs this year in January during a snowstorm. The law of averages alone dictates that hundreds will contract some illness or die of natural causes (compared to any normal city with a population of 2.5 million people), and for many pilgrims death during the Hajj would not be unwelcome. Finally, for bureaucratic comparability, let us say that, with the exception of the diplomats abroad who had to stamp more than a million visas in the pilgrims' passports (many families travel on the same passport), no federal officials, only Virginia state officials, can be involved in the administration of this event.

This brief description may give some inkling of the magnitude of the undertaking for the Saudi government, which must administer the Hajj with a developing bureaucracy that has been in existence in a modern form for slightly more than sixty-five years. Viewed from such a perspective, one might well ask how the Saudis have been able to administer the Hajj with so relatively few problems when more advanced bureaucracies would be unable to cope.

THE HAJJ SERVICE INDUSTRY

The first part of the answer is that the Saudis did not nationalize Hajj administration but left it largely in the hands of those in the private sector who had traditionally administered it from earliest times. Although everyone in the Hijaz seems to be involved in one way or another in the Hajj service industry, individuals whose families have been providing these services for centuries retain the main responsibility for guiding the Hajjis through the rites; arranging for food, lodging, and transportation; and seeing after their general welfare while they are in the kingdom. They are divided into four tightly knit guilds—the *mutawwifin* (singular *mutawwif*), the *wukala'* (singular *wakil*), the *adilla'* (singular *dalil*), and the *Zamzamia* (singular *Zamzami*).

The mutawwifin (the name comes from *tawaf*) form the most important guild; they have responsibility for getting the Hajjis to Saudi Arabia and remain responsible for them while they are in Makkah and its environs. Closely allied with the mutawwifin are the wukala' ("deputies" in Arabic), who generally live in Jiddah. They meet the incoming Hajjis at Jiddah's airport and its sea terminals as well as those pilgrims traveling overland and care for them until they depart for Makkah and then return to Jiddah before embarking for home. The adilla' ("agents" in Arabic) care for the Hajjis during their stay in al-Madinah, and the Zamzamia now generally have contractual arrangements to assist the mutawwifin. Traditionally, they provided Hajjis with water from the sacred well of Zamzam, a huge task considering the number of Hajjis.

Each mutawwif and his associates from the other guilds are in charge of Hajjis from a given country or region. Often, the mutawwif family originally came from that country; in any case, the mutawwif and his staff know the local languages and customs of the Hajjis under their care. Mutawwifin or members of their staffs usually travel to their assigned countries annually in order to work out administrative details with local governments and make arrangements for those wishing to make the Hajj that year. Their high degree of specialization, based on generations of experience, enables the Hajj to proceed with a minimum of chaos.

Another important part of the Hajj service industry is internal transportation. It is difficult to imagine that, within living memory, the kingdom's primary means of transportation was the camel. Although mechanized overland transport had become common in many parts of the world by the time the Al Sauds conquered the Hijaz, it was rudimentary in Saudi Arabia until after World War II. In 1946, King Abd al-Aziz's finance minister, Abdallah Sulayman, created the Arabian Transport Company for the primary purpose of transporting Hajjis inside the kingdom by bus and motorcar. In 1948, a second company was established, the Bakhashab Transport Company (later named the Tawhid Transport Company). These two companies soon monopolized virtually all internal Hajj transportation, leading the government to create the *Niqabat al-Sayarat* (Transportation Syndicate) with exclusive right to carry foreign Hajjis to and from the holy places. The syndicate is administered by the Transportation Department of the Hajj Ministry and can be joined by any Saudi company that can supply a minimum of one hundred buses and twenty sedans, all of which must pass government inspection.

Public Regulation of the Hajj Service Industry

Before the Saudis conquered the Hijaz in 1924, the operations of the Hajj service industry were entirely laissez-faire, and a major aim was self-enrichment. Since then, however, the Saudis have made a concerted effort to ensure that the Hajj is administered fairly and equitably. Through tight regulation, they have transformed various segments of the Hajj service industry into what the West would consider public utilities—privately operated but publicly regulated.

Over the years, the government has issued regulations defining the duties and responsibilities of the guilds and other purveyors of Hajj services as well as the fees they receive for their services. To ensure that they do not try to extract more than the set amount from unsuspecting Hajjis, the government itself collects the fees and then pays the guildsmen on the basis of how many Hajjis they have serviced. It has also established procedures for hearing complaints against the Hajj service industry. The Hajj Ministry provides direct services for Hajjis, including housing, food markets, water, mosques, and postal service (this last in conjunction with the Ministry of Posts, Telegraphs, and Telephones).

OTHER PUBLIC ADMINISTRATIVE RESPONSIBILITIES

In addition to regulating the private-sector Hajj service industry and providing limited services, the government has many other direct administrative tasks. These responsibilities are coordinated at the highest level by the Supreme Hajj Committee. Established in 1966, the committee is a linear descendent of the Committee for the Administration of the Hajj, which dates from the earliest days of Saudi rule in the Hijaz, and its successor, the Committee on the Hajj and the Mutawwifin.

The Supreme Hajj Committee is chaired by the amir of Makkah (governor of the Western Province) and made up of principal representatives in the Hijaz of the ministries of Health, Interior, Hajj, and other government agencies. It serves as the main steering committee for the supervision of all governmental Hajj activities. The committee convenes each year several months in advance of the Hajj (usually right after Ramadan) to plan what needs to be done that year and meets again right after the Hajj to evaluate the results and make recommendations for the future.

The scope of the administrative responsibilities is staggering. For example, the Foreign Ministry must issue hundreds of thousands of Hajj visas to foreign pilgrims, and during the rites offers protocol services to VIP Hajjis and

Hajj delegations from all over the Muslim world. The problems associated with Hajj visas can be much more difficult than one might imagine. Many West African Hajjis literally walk across the continent, stopping for as long as a year or so to work and raise money to pay expenses. Many end up at Khartoum, Sudan, with no visas to the kingdom or travel documents. They not only swamp the Saudi embassy but their own embassies as well.

Likewise, internal transportation entails far more than the motorcar syndicate. The network of paved roads that now blankets the kingdom was originally designed with the Hajj in mind. The first segment to be completed, in 1958, was between Jiddah and al-Madinah, a major Hajj route.

Traffic control, primarily the responsibility of the Ministry of Interior, reaches epic proportions during the Hajj, particularly during the Nafra, when all 2.5 million Hajjis try to rush from 'Arafat to Mina. By comparison, imagine twenty Super Bowl or World Cup soccer games getting out at the same time and place and everyone wanting to leave in the same direction. The Saudis have built more than a dozen multilane highways to facilitate the Nafra and installed the latest traffic control technology, including closed-circuit television, to monitor traffic. Still, the job is Herculean, and traffic tie-ups can last for hours.

External travel, which is no less a burden, has greatly evolved over the years. Throughout the nineteenth and early twentieth centuries, most Hajjis came overland by camel caravan— although before the Hijaz Railway was destroyed in World War I by Lawrence of Arabia and others, increasing numbers of Hajjis from the Fertile Crescent and Turkey used it to travel to al-Madinah. The famous narrow-gauge railroad was built with donations from all over the Muslim world. Today, remains of rolling stock can still be seen at al-'Ula, north of al-Madinah, sitting silently as if waiting for the rails to be relaid so that the trains can be on their way.[3]

The camel caravans were grand affairs that took weeks or months to arrive. The two most famous set out each year from Egypt and Syria, replete with colorful banners and *mahmals* (ceremoniously decorated camel litters). The Egyptian caravan also bore the Kiswa, the black and gold embroidered cloth that covers the Ka'ba and is replaced each year before the Hajj. It is now made in a factory in Makkah.

By the time the Al Sauds first began to administer the Hajj, most Hajjis came by sea, and Jiddah was the primary port of entry. Still later, air travel became and remains the most popular means of travel, although the network of paved roads through the Middle East has revived overland travel. In 1945, King Abd al-Aziz established Saudi Arabian Airlines (now Saudia), with the transport of Hajjis his primary motive. The airline, originally managed by

Trans World Airlines, was incorporated in 1963 as a semi-autonomous public corporation under the Directorate of Civil Aviation in the Ministry of Defense and Aviation. Since then, it has become the largest air carrier in the Middle East, and its familiar green livery is seen in airports around the world. During the Hajj season, Saudia charters hundreds of flights to transport Hajjis to and from the entire Muslim world. Saudi Arabia has agreements with other Muslim states to share this considerable charter business.

As Hajj air traffic increased, Saudi Arabia was required to construct one of the world's largest and most modern airports at Jiddah, still the principal port of entry for the Hajj. One of the Hajj pavilions at the airport is the world's largest single-story structure under one roof. The airport, which took many years to build, now accommodates during the Hajj season more takeoffs and landings than any other airport in the world.

With so much international traffic, the Saudis must take special measures to ensure that all Hajjis arrive in time to make the Hajj: One must be standing on the plain of 'Arafat at sunset on Standing Day, the ninth of Dhu al-Hijja, for it to be valid. Thus, Saudi land borders are closed to Hajj traffic on the first of Dhu al-Hijja, Jiddah seaport on the fifth, and Jiddah's King Abd al-Aziz International Airport on the sixth.

Public health and sanitation procedures at the Hajj developed separately from other administrative procedures but are no less important. The first modern Hajj health regulations were introduced in the nineteenth century by Western powers concerned about the westward spread of cholera. Beginning about 1817, Hajjis from Indonesia and India brought the disease to Makkah, where it was transmitted to Hajjis from North Africa and from there spread to Europe and the Western Hemisphere. Cholera epidemics reached England in 1831 and the United States the following year.

In 1857, the first International Sanitary Conference was convened in Paris to seek ways to prevent the Hajj from being a conduit for the spread of cholera. In 1892, the first of a series of international sanitary conventions regulating the health aspects of the Hajj was signed in Venice. The Venice Convention and subsequent conventions placed a great deal of the responsibility on the countries of origin. In 1894, quarantine stations were established at al-Tur in the Sinai and Kamaran Island in the Red Sea.

In 1926, an international convention was signed that granted the responsibility for administering the health aspects of the Hajj to the Paris Office of International Hygiene, one of the precursors of the World Health Organization. The Saudis, who had just come to power in the Hijaz, resented this international administration as an infringement of their sovereignty. They were in no position to protest, however, for they did not have the capability to take on the responsibility themselves. Finally, in 1957, the World Health Organization transferred full responsibility for health and sanitation at the Hajj to the Saudi government.

It is an awesome responsibility. Preventive medical procedures such as requiring vaccination certificates must be observed to control the spread of contagious diseases among the roughly 1.8 million foreign Hajjis, but at the same time health officials must be careful not to impose unreasonable restrictions on any Muslim to perform what is considered a God-given right and religious duty. The Saudi Health Ministry must also perform curative medical services, and has established an elaborate infrastructure, including first-aid stations, field hospitals, and mobile health units.

The Health Ministry, in cooperation with Makkah municipal authorities, also provides sanitary outdoor facilities for the estimated 1.5 million animals sacrificed on 'Id al-Adha and enforces health standards during transportation of the animals by the Saudi Livestock Transportation Company. The standards must not only meet modern sanitary requirements but also the Quranic injunction that all the animals be without blemish.

Disposal of this enormous number of animals after the sacrifice is also a problem. In years past, to prevent spoilage in the hot sun, great pits were dug where meat not able to be consumed immediately was buried. Today, much of the meat is saved for distribution to the poor and needy throughout the Muslim world, a task administered by the Use of Sacrificial Meat Project of the Islamic Development Bank. (The bank distributes a booklet in nine languages to Hajjis explaining the project.) In support of the project, the kingdom has built and maintains extensive slaughterhouse and cold-storage facilities near Mina, employing about 12,000 people, of whom about 8,600 are butchers and 350 veterinarians.

Beginning in 1983, the project distributed the meat of 63,000 sheep throughout Saudi Arabia and neighboring countries. Today, it distributes to more than twenty-three Muslim countries and is preparing to add the newly independent Muslim countries of Eastern Europe and Central Asia to the distribution list as well as Muslim minorities in other countries.

The bank now buys annually about 500,000 sheep and 14,000 cows and camels and contracts with a Saudi firm to sell vouchers to Hajjis authorizing the project to perform the sacrifice on their behalf. The voucher, which serves as proof of the sacrifice, costs about SR 430 (about $115, the price of a sheep). Following the sacrifice, the animals are processed and stored until they can be distributed. The procedure has been approved by Saudi religious authorities in a fatwa; and while perhaps not cost-effective, is a fitting gesture to the sacred rite of Hajj.[4]

The greatest health hazards at the Hajj are the advanced age of many of the Hajjis and the heat of the desert climate to which all Hajjis must be exposed for long periods. When the Hajj occurs in the summer months, temperatures can exceed 50 degrees C (123 degrees F). Huge crowds are also health risks, creating accidents that involve trampling and being run down by vehicles. The most accident-prone areas are the Maqam Ibrahim in the Haram Mosque, the roads from 'Arafat to Muzdalifa during the Nafra, and the areas around the jamaras during the stone throwing.

Health administration has improved dramatically in the past twenty years, but complaints continue to be aired each year. Nevertheless, considering the extremely adverse environmental conditions—a desert climate where Hajjis spend considerable periods outside, the advanced age of many Hajjis, and the huge crowds—it is a tribute to the Saudi government that conditions are as good as they are.

One of the most important tasks facing the Saudis is the internal security of the Hajj. With pilgrims coming from all over the Muslim world, the Hajj provides a natural platform for espousing political causes before the single largest live Muslim audience. During the protracted confrontation between the Saudis and President Nasser in the 1960s, Egypt attempted to create incidents at the Hajj and raise questions about the Saudis' fitness to administer it. Until the collapse of the Soviet Union, Soviet Hajjis were also used to promote state policies.

Throughout the 1980s, the Iranians made concerted efforts to disrupt the Hajj and discredit Saudi guardianship of the holy places. Each year, Iranian Hajjis demonstrated, passed out anti-Saudi literature, and tried to inflame anti-Saudi sentiment among the Hajjis. The situation came to a head in 1987 when four hundred Hajjis were killed in violent demonstrations instigated by the Iranian government. The incident backfired for Iran, however, as most of the Muslim world blamed Iran for the incident and for desecrating the Hajj.[5] To the Saudis, the riots were not only a political provocation but also a religious desecration.

In the 1990s, with international travel easier and militant Islamic revivalist movements expanding throughout the Muslim world, increasing numbers of young, politicized Muslims, supported by states such as Iran, have sought to make political statements at the Hajj, some contemplating acts of violence. If anything, the threat to internal security has increased over the past few years. Concerns over increasing threats of political violence and the sheer growth in numbers of those seeking to make the Hajj have finally forced the government to take the unprecedented step of limiting the number of attendees. The government currently encourages Saudis and resident aliens who have made the Hajj not to go every year and has established quotas for foreign Hajjis. Quotas again raise the dilemma between the necessity to protect the Hajj from provocateurs (and overcrowding) and the right of all able Muslims to make the Hajj. Most Muslim countries, concurring with the Saudi desire not to profane the Hajj with political activism, have cooperated in seeking to screen out potential troublemakers at the point of departure.

Abd al-Aziz's two avowed purposes in conquering the Hijaz were to open the Hajj to all Muslims and reform its administration, which he felt was corrupt under the Hashimites. The Saudis have taken their responsibilities very seriously in the intervening years. Throughout their entire guardianship of the Muslim holy places, the Saudis have strived to uphold their sanctity and accessibility to all Muslims.

In the beginning, many Muslim countries feared that the zealous Wahhabis would allow only the strict Hanbali interpretation of the Hajj rites; and Saudi religious leaders did ban some practices, such as the mahmals, which they believed were not strictly in accordance with the Shari'a. In an Islamic congress called by Abd al-Aziz during the 1926 Hajj, however, delegates resolved that only the religious authorities of each school of Islamic jurisprudence had the right to adjudicate for their followers which specific rites to observe. This injunction applied to Shi'as as well, and after an initial reluctance, Persia, which governed the largest number of Shi'as, became convinced that its Hajjis would not be discriminated against.

D. Van der Meulen, who was for many years the Dutch consul in Jiddah and responsible for Dutch East Indian Hajjis, wrote in the 1950s that, as the Saudis made the Hajj a comparatively easy, safe, and healthy undertaking, they would make it spiritually cheap as well.[6] The opposite seems to be the case. Muslims seeking to fulfill their obligations to God have come in ever-increasing numbers since World War II to what continues to be the greatest experience of their lifetimes. A 1972 study by a British consulting firm estimated that by the year 2006, the Hajj would reach 3 million, the maximum extent possible based on existing land area at 'Arafat and Mina.[7] The number has almost been reached a decade early.

The Saudis have long anticipated the dramatic rise in numbers. In the 1950s, both the Prophet's Mosque in al-Madinah and the Haram Mosque in Makkah were enlarged—the latter, including the adjoining hills of al-Safa and al-Marwa, to hold a capacity of more than 300,000 worshipers. Today, studies are underway to explore further expansion of the Hajj areas. No one knows what the future of the Hajj will be like. But unlike political and economic institutions that have come and gone in the Middle East for centuries, the Hajj, despite all its administrative changes, is the most likely institution in Saudi Arabia to endure.

7

Saudi Foreign and National Security Policies

The consensual nature of Saudi society often makes its decision-making process appear disjointed and haphazard. When no strong consensus is present, major decisions can be deferred for years. As we have seen, however, there is a consistency to Saudi policy making, born of a combination of Islamic precepts and environmental conditioning, that is quite remarkable. Foreign and national security policies are no exception. They are held together by a powerful perception of the world and the Saudi place in it.

The Saudi World View

The Saudi perception of the world is influenced by two strong themes: an extraordinary cultural self-assurance based on a clear sense of Islamic heritage and tribally based self-identity, and a heightened sense of insecurity based on the historical experience of an insular people surrounded by enemies.[1] These two themes give a unique Saudi cast to three basic Arab attitudes toward international relations, which the kingdom otherwise shares with its fellow Arabs: pan-Arabism, pan-Islamism, and relations with the West.

Pan-Arabism, or secular Arab nationalism, is a relatively recent phenomenon. It is basically the rediscovery of a common Arab heritage rechanneled into the Western concept of state nationalism. The movement began in large part as a reaction to Western military, political, economic, and intellectual penetration of the region, which began with the Napoleonic invasion of Egypt in 1799. It reached its apogee during the 1960s under the charismatic influence of Egypt's President Nasser.

The modern pan-Islamic movement, which also gained momentum in the nineteenth and early twentieth centuries, was a similar attempt to revitalize the Muslim world politically and spiritually in order to enable it to withstand the onslaught of alien secular ideas and ideologies from the West. In the process, a few pan-Islamic writers took liberties with Islamic doctrine to make it more "relevant" to contemporary times.

The Saudi experience with the pan-Arab and pan-Islamic movements was very different from that of most other Arab and Muslim societies. Having never been under colonial domination, the Saudis, particularly Najdis, never lost their sense of Arab identity and consequently never needed to rediscover it. Arab identity in Saudi Arabia is not based primarily on historic, linguistic, cultural, or even religious heritage, important as they are, but on bloodlines. Most Saudis can trace their ancestry as far back as recorded history and their tribal genealogy even farther. The knowledge of their identity has given most Saudis a self-assurance that is unmatched in much of the Middle East. Identity crises, common among Western-educated elites from traditional societies, are rare in Saudi Arabia. This self-assurance has stood the Saudis in good stead in dealing with the West, but it has also had a down side. To some of the kingdom's neighbors who are equally proud of their lineage, it can seem cold and unfeeling.

Perceptions of pan-Islam are also quite different in the kingdom. First, most Saudis have a proprietary attitude toward Islam, which began in the kingdom and is recorded in Arabic, which also originated in the Arabian peninsula. Second, the Saudi Islamic revival of Shaykh Muhammad ibn Abd al-Wahhab was not the result of an anti-Western backlash. It was an entirely indigenous movement that occurred a half-century before Napoleon invaded Egypt.

Saudi perceptions of pan-Islam were substantially strengthened in the 1920s, when Abd al-Aziz occupied the Hijaz with the holy cities of Makkah and al-Madinah. As guardians of the two holiest sites in Islam, the Saudis have assumed an added responsibility as defenders of the Islamic way of life throughout the Muslim world. It is in this context that one must view the title adopted by King Fahd in 1986: Khadim al-Haramayn, or "Custodian of the Two Holy Places."

Finally, the Saudi experience with Western powers is very different from that of most other Arab and Islamic states because the kingdom never experienced nineteenth- and twentieth-century European colonial domination. As a result, Saudis never developed a political xenophobia toward the West as other Arab and Islamic states did. When Saudi xenophobia toward the West appears, it is generally focused on the threat of Western secularism to Islamic society, not on the threat of political domination.

Without the psychological baggage of a people subjugated by Western colonialism, the Saudi view of the world conforms far more closely to the classical Islamic view. This is basically a bipolar world composed of *Dar al-Islam*, or the territory under divine (Islamic) law, and *Dar al-Harb*, the territory of war—that is, outside the rule of God's law.[2] One can see how closely the bipolar world of the cold war could be overlaid conceptually on the Islamic model. Communist regimes were atheistic and could be relegated to Dar al-Harb.

Moreover, Saudi cooperation with the Christian West in combating the threat of atheistic Communism to the Muslim world could also be made to conform to the classical model, for within Dar al-Islam are not only Muslims but also other monotheists subscribing to a divinely inspired revelation. They are known as *Ahl al-Kitab*, or "People of the Book." Sura 2:62 of the Quran states, "Lo! Those who believe (in that which was revealed unto thee, Muhammad), and those who are Jews and Christians and Sabeans [Zoroastrians or Parsees]— whoever believeth in God and the Last Day and doeth right—surely their regard is with their Lord, and there shall be no fear come upon them, neither shall they grieve."

The overlay of the classical Islamic model and the bipolar world of the cold war was not an exact fit. A major problem with the analogy is that, in classical Islam, other "Peoples of the Book" were under Islamic military and political protection, whereas in the twentieth century it has been the other way around. Nevertheless, it was close enough for King Faysal to articulate basic Saudi foreign-policy principles in terms of classical Islamic political theory. Conceptually, he did not include the Christian West in the Dar al-Harb but did include Israel, taking pains to distinguish between Judaism, which is recognized by Islam, and Zionism, which he castigated as a secular, anti-Islamic political doctrine. Characteristically, Saudi opposition to Israel has been fueled as much by a religious issue as by secular political issues—the 1967 Israeli occupation of east Jerusalem and the Aqsa Mosque, the third holiest site in Sunni Islam after Makkah and al-Madinah.

To Communism and Zionism, Faysal added imperialism as an enemy of Islam. In this way, he could oppose Western policies inimical to the Muslim world and separate them from Western efforts to combat Communism.

Although the foreign and national security policy issues confronting Saudi Arabia have changed drastically since Faysal's day, the overall policy framework, a modified form of the classical Islamic model of international relations, remains intact. Using this model enables a number of confusing elements of Saudi foreign and national security policies to come into better perspective. For example, Saudis have never had much affinity for the Third World and what has been known as north-south dialogue. Despite their stated opposition to imperialism, they have always been more concerned with the distinction between the God-fearing and the godless than between the haves and have-nots.

A word of caution should be added. One must look with flexibility at the Saudi world view. It is a perception, not a blueprint for policy action. Saudi Arabia is no different from any other country in viewing issues in international relations in terms of their national interests, not as part of a rigid formula dictating a set response.

A second major perceptual ingredient in the Saudi world view is a highly developed "encirclement syndrome." It is a characteristic among insular peoples surrounded by sand or seas to develop the perception of being encircled by enemies. The Saudi historical experience certainly justifies this perception. Since World War II, virtually every one of the kingdom's neighbors has at one time or another been considered an enemy—Hashimite Jordan and Iraq, whose royal families were forced into exile by King Abd al-Aziz; radical republican Iraq since the overthrow of the monarchy in 1958; Zionist Israel; republican Iran; the PLO when it sided with Iraq in the Kuwait war; Nasserist Egypt; the once pro-Communist and now Islamist Sudan; Communist Ethiopia under Mengistu; leftist Somalia under Siad Barre; Nasserist North Yemen in the 1960s; and Marxist South Yemen in the 1970s and 1980s. There have also been border disputes with Oman, Yemen, the United Arab Emirates, and Qatar and with Britain as protecting power in the lower Gulf, from their entry in the early nineteenth century until 1971.

The long-standing Saudi encirclement syndrome has played a major role in Saudi foreign policy and its search for national security. At the same time, it stands in sharp contrast to the self-assurance bred of a strong sense of self-identity. The anomaly of these two seemingly incompatible themes existing side by side has created an ambivalence in Saudi foreign and national security policies that is not likely to change in the foreseeable future.

The Evolution of Saudi Foreign Policy

Saudi foreign-policy horizons expanded slowly. It was not until during and after World War II that they extended past the Arabian peninsula. Perhaps the first, and certainly the most dramatic, instance of expanded Saudi political horizons was the famous meeting between King Abd al-Aziz and President Roosevelt aboard the USS *Quincy* in the Great Bitter Lake on February 14, 1945. The meeting cemented strong U.S.-Saudi relations that have continued to the present.[3]

In the 1960s, secular Arab nationalism swept the Arab world. Radical Arab nationalists, personified by Egypt's President Nasser, castigated both Israel and the West as common enemies. The Saudis shared the Arab world's sense of injustice at the creation of Israel, but they did not share its secular socialist concept of Arabism. More important, the Saudis saw atheistic Communism as an even greater threat to the Muslim way of life than Zionism was, and they looked to the West as the last defense of the Muslim world. Although stridently anti-Zionist, particularly after the 1967 Arab-Israeli war, Saudi Arabia maintained a low profile in Arab politics. During most of the 1960s, King Faysal and President Nasser engaged in a political confrontation that took on a military dimension in the Yemen civil war (1962–70). The Saudis supported the

Figure 22. King Abd al-Aziz and President Roosevelt aboard the USS *Quincy,* 1945. Photo courtesy of the Roosevelt Library.

Yemeni royalists against the republican government, which was propped up by some 70,000 Egyptian troops.

Radical Arab nationalism declined in the 1970s. At the same time, the energy crisis of 1973–74 propelled the kingdom into the role of a major oil power. As befitted their new status, the Saudis began to take a more active role in both regional politics and international economic and petroleum affairs. This included a more active role in the Arab-Israeli dispute. During the 1973 Arab-Israeli war, King Faysal led the Arab oil boycott against the United States and the Netherlands. It is an open question whether Faysal would have levied the embargo if President Nixon had not announced his decision to give $2.2 billion in military aid to Israel after promising Faysal in a personal communication that the United States would be evenhanded during the war. (An embargo had been levied in the 1967 war, but in a buyer's market it had little effect. Moreover, in 1967, King Faysal continued to ship jet fuel to U.S. forces in Vietnam, which were fighting against Communism.) The king felt that Nixon's announcement was a personal betrayal, just as he believed that President Truman's support for partitioning Palestine had broken the pledge made by President Roosevelt to Faysal's father that the United States would not act on the issue without consulting King Abd al-Aziz. In 1948, Faysal had wanted his father to break diplomatic relations with the United States; in 1973, he levied the Arab oil embargo.

The Camp David Accords and subsequent Egyptian-Israeli Treaty of 1979 were considered a disaster by the Saudis. They believed that President Sadat had not only broken Arab consensus but was seduced into a separate peace for nothing more concrete than vague promises of Palestinian autonomy. The subsequent breakdown of the autonomy talks seemed to justify their fears. In 1981, Prince Fahd, then Saudi heir apparent, sought to restart the peace process outside the moribund Camp David formula by announcing an eight-point plan for a comprehensive peace. The Fahd Plan broke new ground by tacitly recognizing Israel through affirmation of the right of all states in the area to live in peace. The original plan was rejected by the Arabs at a foreign ministers' conference in 1981 but was adopted in modified form the following year at an Arab summit in Morocco. The opportunity to exploit Arab consensus was spurned by the United States and Israel, however, and the plan went nowhere. Thereafter, the Saudis, although still active in the Arab-Israeli peace process, no longer sought a major leadership role.

Just as the kingdom was developing a more comprehensive foreign policy, a series of events significantly changed a number of the basic assumptions on which it was based. First, the demise of Communism and secular Arab nationalism as ideologies of revolutionary change has greatly reduced the political threat to the kingdom from the left. Second, the rise of rival revolutionary Islamic political doctrines, supported in large measure by republican Iran, has undoubtedly created a challenge for Saudi Arabia's Islamic foreign policies.

Up to 1979, the Saudis viewed their primary political threat (other than Zionism) as coming from the left—radical Arab regimes and international Communism. This perception was totally altered by the Islamic revolution in Iran. The revolution not only upset the balance of power in the Gulf but also changed the terms of reference of Saudi foreign policy. Up to 1980, Saudi Arabia was virtually alone among Middle East states to champion an Islamic world order. The Islamic revolution in Iran created a new threat from the right—a challenge to the kingdom's Islamic legitimacy.

The threat was quickly given form and substance by Iran's resort to terrorism and subversion in the Gulf and elsewhere. The Saudis had been suspicious of Iranian intentions in the Gulf long before the fall of the shah and were convinced that Iran harbored ambitions to extend its hegemony throughout the Gulf. From the Saudi perspective, it was virtually impossible to distinguish between the imperial Iranian ambitions of the shah and the universalist Islamic foreign-policy goals professed by his successors.

Iran saw itself in competition with Saudi Arabia, not only in the Gulf but for leadership of the entire Muslim world. It quickly began to challenge all aspects of the kingdom's Islamic policies, using the most provocative means possible, particularly at the annual Hajj, where Iran attempted to call into question Saudi fitness to administer the holy rite by instigating uprisings led by Iranian pilgrims.

Following the collapse of the Soviet Union in 1991, Iran moved quickly to create a position of influence in the former Soviet Islamic republics of Central Asia, seeking to neutralize Saudi influence. In fact, Saudi policy there and elsewhere was not based on competing with Iran but on propagating the faith. Although this attitude did not always sit well with recipient countries more interested in financial aid than spiritual succor, it is an indication of the single-mindedness of Saudi Islamic foreign policies.

The revolutionary Islamic threat has expanded beyond the threat of Iran. With Iran's support, Islamist revolutionaries have organized throughout the Arab world, many of them mutually reinforced in their sense of mission by networking with others, particularly veterans who fought against the Soviets with the Afghan mujahidin. Ironically, Saudi Arabia was a major financial supporter of the mujahidin, and private Saudis are still major supporters of radical Islamist groups. With the fragmentation of regional politics since the collapse of the Soviet Union, the revolutionary Islamist threat to all moderate countries in the region has expanded; and in the absence of any other credible ideology with which to channel political disaffection and protest, it is likely to remain for a long time.

The end of the cold war has also created a conceptual challenge for Saudi foreign policy. The real world is no longer bipolar but highly fragmented, making conformity of Saudi foreign policy with the classical Islamic bipolar model of the world more difficult (although not impossible). On the other hand, the world view of the new breed of Islamist revolutionaries in the region has become much simpler, for they can equate Dar al-Harb with antireligious (as they see it) Western secularism and all secular (by their standards) governments in the Middle East.

One real problem throughout the entire Muslim world in recent years is that the language of Islam has become the idiom of all political dialogue. (Even thoroughly secular Saddam Hussein called for jihad in the Kuwait war.) It is thus much more difficult to sort out truly Islamic politics from what is simply business as usual.

The kingdom has always opposed Western secularism; but with the social dislocations of rapid modernization and runaway population growth throughout the region, the threat of the religious right both inside and outside the country looms larger. There is a real danger that militant Islamists will seek to promote political opposition to the regime by blaming it for introducing secularism into the kingdom. With threats from secular modernism and militant Islamism, Saudi foreign policy in the future will undoubtedly continue to search for a balance between accommodation with the West for the technology and security it affords and the fundamental Islamic principles of the revival movement of Shaykh Muhammad ibn Abd al-Wahhab. This is not a new phenomenon. It is essentially the same dilemma faced by King Faysal a quarter-century ago and by his father, King Abd al-Aziz, a quarter-century before that.

Gulf stability is another major goal of Saudi foreign policy. It was not Iran's perceived threat to orthodox Islam that convinced the Saudis of the need to cooperate more closely with other Gulf countries in the Arabian peninsula but the Iran-Iraq war, which broke out in September 1980. Although the Saudis and their smaller neighbors had long shared oil interests, Saudi foreign policy and security interests generally focused elsewhere before that time. For almost a decade, there had been some talk of a Gulf regional organization, but nothing had come of it, in part because none of the lower Gulf states wished to include Iran or Iraq.

The mutual security threat emanating from the Iran-Iraq war was a major catalyst in the creation of the Gulf Cooperation Council (GCC) in May 1981.[4] The fact that the Arab Gulf countries began thereafter regularly to coordinate policies of mutual interest greatly enhanced the degree of regional cooperation. Thus, from the Saudi perspective, the GCC has become a major instrument of its Gulf policy. (The headquarters of the GCC is located in Riyadh.) Moreover, enhanced cooperation among the GCC states also helped to alleviate resentment over what some of the kingdom's neighbors felt were paternalistic Saudi policies toward them, mixed with neglect.

This new regional cooperation did not prevent a border incident from briefly souring Saudi-Qatari relations. In September 1992, a clash took place at a small Qatari border post in which two Qataris were killed and one taken prisoner by the Saudis. The incident was officially resolved at a meeting between the rulers of the two countries the following December, but feelings still run high.

Despite some continuing bilateral sensitivities, however, the Saudis have succeeded in developing a cohesive Gulf policy. Thus, by the mid-1990s, Saudi foreign policy had reemerged as a fairly comprehensive mix of responses to its expanding Gulf, Arabian peninsula, Middle East, Muslim world, and global interests.

THE SEARCH FOR SAUDI SECURITY

For Saudi Arabia, security and survival have always been one and the same. The Arabian peninsula was a violent place long before Western technology brought warfare to new heights. Moreover, vestiges of that violent world exist within living memory. A Saudi friend once recounted his grandmother's favorite story about a tribal incident before World War I. During a raid by a rival clan, she fled her family's tent carrying a box of gold coins. One of the raiders chased her for the coins, but as he reached for them, she picked up a stone, struck him a fatal blow, and escaped. Years later, my friend had the story confirmed by a member of the rival clan, whose uncle was in the raid. The uncle said that the raiders had indeed seen her hit their clansman with the stone but, wrongly thinking he was trying to molest her, believed he got what he deserved and therefore did not give chase. It is hard to imagine that such a raid took place in the same century as the push-button Kuwait war of 1990.

To end age-old tribal warfare, King Abd al-Aziz, once he had united the kingdom, demobilized his tribal forces and had no standing army for almost two decades. The Ikhwan, as his tribal army was called, was disbanded after tribal units were involved in the uprising at al-Sibila in 1929. (The king again resorted to tribal levies in 1934 for a brief campaign against Yemen led by his son Faysal.)

With no standing military force, the Saudis were not directly involved in the fighting in World War II. They formally declared war on Germany in 1945 to qualify for membership in the United Nations. They clearly sided with the allies, however, and signed a Lend-Lease agreement with the United States in February 1943.

As a result of the war, King Abd al-Aziz realized that he could no longer continue the luxury of not having a standing army; nor could he rely on tribal levies in an era of modern warfare. He therefore initiated a military development process that continues to the present day.

At the time, he considered the two greatest threats to Saudi national security to be hostile neighbors moving against Saudi oil fields and general threats to overthrow the regime either militarily or through subversion. With the spread of Communism after World War II, those concerns became strongly associated with a larger Soviet threat, both directly and through Soviet clients in the region.

Since the Soviet threat ended in 1991, Iran and Iraq have become greater direct military threats to both the regime and the Saudi oil fields. The Iran-Iraq war and the Iraqi invasion of Kuwait demonstrated beyond all doubt the vital importance of maintaining and upgrading Saudi military forces. Moreover, while the source of the threat has changed drastically since World War II, concern for oil field security and the stability of the regime are still foremost security interests.

The Saudis also continue to be concerned about the security threat from Yemen. The threat of a hostile Communist South Yemen appeared to end when, in May 1990, the two Yemens united. The Saudi perception of a potential security threat was revived, however, when Yemen sided diplomatically with

Iraq in the Kuwait war. The Saudi response was to expel hundreds of thousands of Yemenis from the kingdom, creating hardship for both countries. The Yemenis, mainly unskilled and semiskilled laborers, needed work; and the Saudis needed laborers.

Subsequently, many Yemeni laborers were allowed to return to the kingdom, and in early 1995 the Saudis agreed to negotiate outstanding disputes over the Saudi-Yemeni border. Thus, relations improved to a degree. Nevertheless, the Saudis have not forgotten that Yemen did not support them during the Kuwait war; and when southern Yemen initiated an abortive attempt to dissolve the union with northern Yemen in 1994, Saudi sympathies were with the south.

THE DEVELOPMENT OF MODERN SAUDI ARMED FORCES

After World War II, King Abd al-Aziz established two basic goals for Saudi national security policy: to create a modern Saudi defense force and to create external security relationships with strong, trustworthy powers. He initially accomplished both aims by turning to the United States and Britain to help him create a modern military force. In the process, he hoped to obtain a commitment from them to defend the kingdom.

In 1944, the two countries agreed to send a joint military advisory mission to Saudi Arabia; but due to Anglo-American rivalries extant in the region at the time, they sent separate teams. The British subsequently established a training mission in 1947 to create a lightly mechanized force of 10,000 men. Nevertheless, the Saudis increasingly looked for external security support to the United States as the superpower of the free world, and in 1951 the British mission was phased out.

The first U.S.-Saudi military cooperation agreement was signed in 1945 and provided for a U.S. air base at Dhahran, to be turned over to the kingdom three years after the end of the war. This changeover was to have occurred in March 1949, but with the advent of the cold war, a second agreement was signed the following June that enabled the Americans to remain at Dhahran until 1962.

As a part of the second agreement, a U.S. survey team traveled more than 44,000 miles in the kingdom in the fall of 1949 collecting basic strategic data. It recommended training and equipping a 43,000-man armed force (a 28,000-man army and 15,000-man air force) over five years. Although the recommendation, known as the 1380 Plan, was never formally adopted, it became the first comprehensive plan for building a modern Saudi military force. In 1951, a permanent U.S. Military Training Mission for Saudi Arabia (USMTM) was created, which has become the principal U.S. military training and development organization in the kingdom.[5]

Paralleling the development of a modern military force was the reconstitution of a tribally based paramilitary force. In 1956, remnants of the old tribal Ikhwan army were reconstituted as the Saudi national guard—sometimes known as the White Army because of the flowing white robes (*thaubs*) that the troops wore. With recruitment based on loyalty to the royal family, its original mission was to counterbalance the regular armed forces in a period of rising secular Arab nationalism and revolution throughout the Middle East.

The national guard was originally administered directly under King Saud by a succession of his sons, aided by a small staff. When Faysal took over as prime minister in 1962, he appointed his brother, Prince Abdallah, as commander of the guard, a position he still held in 1995. In 1963, Prince Abdallah turned to the British to create an advisory training mission to modernize the guard. Ten years later, he replaced the British with Americans, who created the U.S.-Saudi Arabian National Guard (SANG) program. The program was kept separate from USMTM in order to avoid becoming involved in long-standing rivalries between the guard and the regular armed forces.

The development of a modern Saudi military establishment has often seemed to proceed by fits and starts. Both training and specific arms purchases have frequently been subjected to intense political pressures (particularly from the United States, the kingdom's major supplier), which have at times undermined military efficiency. If viewed over a forty-five-year period, however, Saudi military development has followed a relatively orderly, consistent process based on a consensus between foreign military advisors and Saudi political and military leaders on how best to meet the defense and security needs of the country.

In the beginning, the value of a Western-trained armed force may not have been entirely appreciated by King Abd al-Aziz. He apparently saw military training programs as secondary to the commitment by Western powers to defend the kingdom. For years, the American embassy in Saudi Arabia kept a list of oral commitments to the security of Saudi Arabia made by every U.S. president from Roosevelt on. For a country where one's word is his bond, those commitments were far more important to Saudi Arabia than most Americans probably realized.

As the world entered the cold war, however, the need for a modern military force became more apparent to the Saudis. For a period in the 1950s, King Saud flirted with Nasserism, apparently enamored with the charismatic vision of Egypt's president. He established a large Egyptian military training mission in the kingdom. Saudi relations with the United States grew ever stormier, leading eventually to the cancellation of U.S. base rights at Dhahran in 1962. Even then, however, the king wanted USMTM to remain a sign of the U.S. commitment to defend Saudi Arabia.

The Yemen civil war (1962–70) convinced King Faysal that the kingdom must become more committed to building a modern military force. In 1963, the Saudi Defense Ministry, working closely with USMTM, produced a second, more comprehensive development plan. Known as Armed Forces Defense Plan No. 1, it became the main blueprint for military development in the 1960s.

The plan failed to address Saudi air defense needs, however, prompting the United States to conduct a major air defense survey for the kingdom. The survey was originally offered by Ambassador Ellsworth Bunker as an incentive to King Faysal to accept U.S. mediation between him and President Nasser over the Yemen civil war. The king agreed, and although the mediation effort failed, he got his air defense survey. Completed in November 1963, it became the basis for the creation of a modern Saudi air force and air defense force.

In the mid-1960s, Prince Sultan, who had been appointed minister of defense and aviation by Faysal in 1962, began to consider a naval expansion program. The Saudi navy had been created in 1957 under the command of the army but still had no mission or organizational structure. In 1968–69, a U.S. survey team made a complete study of Saudi naval needs and recommended a small, two-flotilla navy—one based at Jiddah on the Red Sea and one at Jubayl on the Gulf, with headquarters in Riyadh. As a result, the Saudi Arabian Naval Expansion Plan (SNEP) came into being in 1972 under the direction of USMTM. It was, in fact, the beginning of a modern Saudi naval force.

In 1970, Prince Sultan requested a third comprehensive military development plan, which became known as the Leahy Report (named after U.S. Major General Oswald Leahy, who conducted it). Although the Leahy Report, like its predecessors, was never formally adopted, it became the main development plan for the 1970s. By then, however, unexpected oil wealth made cost no constraint, and Saudi military expansion increased geometrically. The size of the Saudi programs soon came under heavy criticism from the U.S. Congress, which claimed that the United States was inciting an arms race in the Gulf. In fact, most of the expenditures were not for weapons at all but were devoted to military construction, including base housing and other facilities for personnel.

The principal rationale for heavy Saudi military capital expenditures was and remains demographic. Saudi Arabia has a much smaller population than nearly all of its potential adversaries and covers a huge geographical area. Recognizing the kingdom's small manpower pool, the Leahy Report specifically recommended more sophisticated arms, which would create, in effect, a capital-intensive military force rather than a labor-intensive one. The air force received special attention as the only force that could physically defend all Saudi borders simultaneously.

This emphasis on sophisticated weapons systems remains a major consideration in Saudi arms requests. Military purchases in the 1970s exceeded the armed forces' ability to absorb them, but the general principle was no less valid. Spending declined in the 1980s; but as a result of Desert Storm, perhaps the most technologically proficient war in history, the Saudis saw the need to modernize their armed forces further. They therefore placed large orders for additional equipment. From the United States alone they ordered more F-15s, Abrams M-1A2 main battle tanks, Patriot antimissile missiles, Apache helicopters, and an integrated air-defense system known as Peace Shield.

These additional orders have created a new dilemma for the kingdom. With a serious short-term cash flow problem in the 1990s necessitating spending cuts (see chapter 5) and an almost geometric rise in prices for the latest military technology, the Saudis will be hard pressed to put a cap on military spending and modernize at the same time. They may be forced to scale back or draw out arms purchases over a period of years.

In sum, realization of the necessity for a modern military force has come gradually over the years. In the 1967 Arab-Israeli war, King Faysal sent Saudi armor south rather than risk having unprepared troops mauled in modern combat. By the 1973 war, a Saudi battalion was sent to participate, still mainly as a symbolic gesture. In the 1980s, the Iran-Iraq war, which was waged only minutes of flying time away from the kingdom, served as a wake-up call. Saudi air force pilots flew defensive patrols over the Gulf along a perimeter known as the Fahd line and were able to scramble moments after an alert of intruders coming close to the line. In 1991, the Saudis participated in a substantive way in the first large-scale modern warfare they had ever experienced. With accelerated training and logistical support from the United States and other coalition forces, they acquitted themselves very well.

THE ARMED FORCES AND INTERNAL SECURITY

Despite their acknowledged need for modern military capability, the Saudis have always been ambivalent about having a permanent standing military force. This attitude has been reinforced by the record of other Arab regimes, many of which have been overthrown by professional military leaders. Thus, while building up the military with one hand, the government has always limited its capabilities with the other to ensure that it protects rather than threatens the regime. Development of the tribally based Saudi Arabian national guard as a check on the regular armed forces is a case in point.

In earlier stages of military development, maintaining internal security in the armed forces could be done by appointing commanders based on their loyalty to the regime rather than on competence. With a growing need for professional competence, however, this has become increasingly difficult. Thus, the Saudis have begun resorting to more sophisticated methods to maintain security within the armed forces—for example, by commissioning royal princes, particularly into the air force, considered the glamorous branch of service. They have also taken other steps, such as isolating troop units, prohibiting combined force movements as security measures, and seeing to the personal welfare of the officer corps of the various branches.

Security concerns about a professional standing army raise the broader question of general internal security in the kingdom. It may be difficult from a Western perspective to understand how a traditional Islamic monarchy that rejects Western ideas of liberal democracy is not seething with political discontent. In fact, Saudi Arabia is one of the most stable countries in the region. As noted in chapter 1, the source of stability is not so much its political institutions or its generous economic and social welfare programs but the extraordinarily resilient extended family structure of its society. With the role of the family so central, Saudi society is not a class society in the Western sense (with upper, middle, and lower classes) but a modern tribal society with uncles and cousins to whom one can always appeal for a helping hand.

A frequently heard internal security concern of outside observers is the rivalry between Saudi secularists and Islamic fundamentalists. Although the concern has a degree of validity, it ignores some basic cultural and political realities in the kingdom. Secularism as practiced in the West is practically unknown in Saudi Arabia. Culturally, all Saudi society is both Islamic and highly conservative, and in that context even Saudi modernists generally subscribe to the fundamentalist Hanbali school of Islamic jurisprudence. The average Saudi, regardless of family background, personal income, love of the good life, or degree of political influence, tends to be personally very devout.

At the same time, there is a sharp difference of opinion among some Saudis over how strict their compliance to Shari'a civil and criminal codes should be. Some Saudis do feel that the execution of Islamic law is too inflexible. But virtually no one, even the most modernized Saudi, advocates abandoning the Shari'a as the basis of the Saudi Arabian constitutional system or the Wahhabi doctrine of Tawhid (strict monotheism) as the basis of Saudi foreign and domestic policies. Separation of church and state, the basis of Western secularism, would be viewed as not only ludicrous by most Saudis but heretical as well.

The clash between the secularizing influences of modernization and the rejection of secularization by an assertive Islamic society has led to a great deal of political tension over the years. Saudi rulers have always been aware of this dilemma and have sought to keep the two opposing trends in balance. The success of the kingdom's wide-reaching modernization programs, however, has actually made the task all the harder. Currently, the most vocal critics of the regime's development policies belong to a new breed of Saudi Islamists who call for a return to a strict, inflexible application of Islamic law. Calling themselves *Salafiyin*, or "followers of the pious ancestors," they are vociferous and articulate. While denouncing modernization as heretical, they have been quick to adapt modern technology to spread their message. For example, they use tape recorders to disseminate sermons of militant Islamist preachers at home and fax machines to communicate with like-minded Islamists overseas.

To gain more sympathy in the West for their cause, they have linked their criticism of the regime to a denial of human rights. In May 1993, a group of prominent Islamists created the Committee for the Defense of Legitimate Rights.[6] The irony is that the Islamists deny the existence of secular *human* rights, insisting that all rights come from God—hence the use of the phrase "legitimate rights," referring only to rights granted in Islamic law.

Islamist doctrine in Saudi Arabia is primarily the province of the religious elite, or ulama (singular, *alim*), many of whom feel threatened by the secularizing influences of modernization. At the same time, the more puritanical and the more moderate members of the ulama have engaged in vociferous political infighting for years, for the most part unnoted by outside observers until recently. It is hardly a new debate in the kingdom.

The more puritanical ulama have not enjoyed great public support in past years as the government balanced their concerns with those of modernization. More recently, however, they have received more support, particularly among young underemployed or unemployed Saudis. Many of these young supporters are graduates of Muhammad ibn Saud University, an Islamic institution in Riyadh whose curriculum is almost entirely religious studies and offers few other marketable skills. With virtually no openings in the professional religious establishment, its graduates are essentially unemployable. Many have become volunteers with the Committee for Propagating Virtue and Suppressing Evil, or *mutawa'in* (the religious police), and seek to force the population to conform to more strict Islamic social norms.

On November 13, 1995, fiery talk was replaced by violence. Offices of the U.S. training mission to the Saudi Arabian national guard in Riyadh were bombed, killing five Americans and several third-country nationals and wounding nearly sixty people.[7] Two shadowy groups, the Tigers of the Gulf and the Islamic Movement for Change, claimed credit. On June 4, 1996, an even more devastating bomb attack on U.S. military housing near Dhahran killed nineteen Americans. Such direct defiance of government authority cannot be ignored. Nevertheless, the Salafiya movement thus far has neither the mass support nor the organizational skills to mount a serious challenge to the regime, and there is little to indicate that the political system itself is in immediate jeopardy of collapse.

To maintain public order, the government has continued to develop its internal security services. In addition to the national guard, they include the national police and an internal security police, the General Investigations Department under the Ministry of Interior, the coast guard and frontier force under the Ministry of Defense and Aviation, and a national intelligence service.

SAUDI NATIONAL SECURITY AND THE WEST

It has already been noted that King Abd al-Aziz, free of the psychological scars of a colonial past, had few compunctions about seeking a security relationship with Western powers. They were obviously more powerful than his immediate neighbors and, from his perspective, more reliable (or at least less unreliable) as allies. He thus initiated a policy of reliance on the West to protect the kingdom against external military threats, a policy that has continued to the present.

Although the Saudis have relied principally on the United States as their primary source of external security since World War II, the relationship has not been an exclusive one. The Saudis have also accepted military training missions and security assistance from Britain, France, Egypt, and Pakistan and have purchased arms from many countries, including China. Moreover, the Saudi-American security relationship has always been characterized by a great deal of ambivalence. The United States has consistently sought to limit its military commitment to Saudi Arabia in order to avoid becoming entangled in local disputes beyond the scope of its interests in the region. That, in turn, has caused the Saudis to call into question the strength of the U.S. commitment to protect the kingdom. Assuaging Saudi anxieties has been a major element of the relationship.

The Saudis are highly sensitive to any perceived infringement of their sovereignty as a result of military cooperation with a powerful Western state. They have sought to avoid accusations from their own citizens and other Arab states that the kingdom has relinquished any portion of its sovereignty by granting concessions such as base rights, pre-positioning of equipment, or blanket overflight privileges.

The Saudis have also resented overweening U.S. support for Israel over the years, beginning with the major U.S. role in the creation of Israel in 1948 and the failure to consult the Saudis as President Roosevelt had given his word the Americans would do. This resentment has mounted over the years as Israel and its American supporters have treated U.S.-Saudi and U.S.-Israeli relations as a zero-sum game, particularly in the area of arms sales. Organized U.S. supporters of Israel have systematically lobbied Congress to block or scale down virtually every major Saudi arms request to the United States since 1956 or to compensate Israel with additional arms sales as a quid pro quo.

The degree of anxiety and resentment that U.S. Middle East policies have generated in Saudi Arabia has waxed and waned over the years. It was obviously high in 1948 and again during the 1967 and 1973 Arab-Israeli wars. Anxiety also ran high as a result of what was seen as a U.S. failure to help preserve the monarchy in Iran in 1979–80 (the Saudis were worried about what the United States would do if the kingdom faced a similar threat) and the 1986 U.S. offer of air-to-surface missiles to the revolutionary regime in Tehran in return for the freeing of U.S. hostages in Lebanon.

On the other hand, the sale of F-15s to the Saudis in 1978 and electronic early-warning E-3 AWACS (Airborne Warning and Communications System) aircraft in 1981 were high points in the relationship. To the Saudis, they were litmus tests of friendship with a psychological value almost as great as the defense one.

As it turned out, those sales were not the turning point in the relationship that the Saudis had hoped for. In 1985, President Reagan informed King Fahd that the United States could not obtain congressional approval for additional F-15s and an advanced air attack capability it had been trying to get for five years. The Saudis turned to the British, buying Tornado aircraft and other arms in a multibillion-dollar program called al-Yamamah. An even more controversial purchase was fifty to fifty-six Chinese CSS-2 surface-to-surface missiles in 1988 for $3 to $3.5 billion. The Saudis purchased these missiles when arms-sales relations with the United States were at a low point and also out of concern that Iraq and Iran both had long-range missiles while Saudi Arabia did not. Nevertheless, the missiles are obsolete and, because they are conventionally armed, appear to have little strategic value.[8]

After Desert Storm, the United States again agreed to follow-on arms sales. Desert Storm also convinced the Saudis (and other GCC members) of the absolute need for external protection in case of a determined attack by Iran or Iraq (assuming they remain hostile) and of the inadequacy of their previous philosophy of keeping U.S. military forces "over the horizon" until needed. There is considerable doubt that Desert Storm would have gone so well had not the coalition had six months to prepare—a lesson undoubtedly learned by Iran and Iraq as well.

It is difficult to imagine any country other than the United States in the role of external protector in the Gulf, but the mere presence of large numbers of foreign troops in the kingdom cannot help but contribute to continued U.S.-Saudi tensions. Thus, by all indications, consistency and ambivalence will continue to be hallmarks of U.S.-Saudi military relations, and of Saudi national security policy in general, for the foreseeable future.

8

Saudi Arabia in the Twenty-First Century

Saudi Arabia has witnessed a period of unparalleled social, political, and economic change in the twentieth century, at a pace matched by few countries in the world. Over the past century, the regime has created a solid record of achievement in economic, social, and political development. It has succeeded to a remarkable degree in creating a modern economy and bureaucratic structure while maintaining a traditional Islamic society and political system. Furthermore, it has done so without incurring a major revolution or other violent political upheaval so common among rapidly developing countries.

Despite past successes, the challenges Saudi Arabia will face in the twenty-first century in seeking to maintain economic prosperity, political stability, and social harmony are likely to grow at an exponential rate. Just to sustain the current level of development will require the government to use in the most efficient manner possible the entire resources of the kingdom—human, economic, and political. And with the population explosion, the economy will have to grow at more than 3 percent just to maintain the same per capita income, something it has not done in the last decade.

Prospects for Saudi Social Development

Saudi Arabia's deeply traditional Islamic society appears to be living proof of the assertion that basic social values do not change rapidly over time, no matter how drastic the changes in the social and physical environment. If someone were to invent a time machine that could bring an eighteenth-century Najdi into the present, it would probably be only a matter of weeks before he became a functioning member of society, facing the onslaught of modern life with the same certitude of religious conviction with which he once faced the onslaught of enemy tribal raids. By extension, it seems reasonable to assume that the Islamic social values of the current generation will be shared by its descendants in the next century.

If basic values do not change rapidly, however, basic attitudes do, particularly those that respond to changes in the environment. Few places on earth have witnessed changes in the physical and intellectual environment at the pace that Saudi Arabia has in the twentieth century, and that pace is not likely to slacken in the next. The kingdom has recently created a sort of cultural fairground at Janadriyya, outside Riyadh, to save for future generations the arts, architecture, culture, and customs of the kingdom that were common-place only twenty-five years ago. Since that time, a generation of Saudis have grown up never knowing poverty as their parents did or the necessity of hard work simply for physical survival as their grandparents did. Most children are more familiar with the icons of Disney World than with Arab poetry played to the wail of the *rababa* (a traditional, single-stringed instrument). The genera-tions of the twenty-first century will be even more removed from their his-torical past. The great question of the next century, therefore, is what future generations' attitudes will be toward society, politics, and material wealth.

As mentioned in chapter 7, the greatest existential fact of the modern Saudi social development process since the discovery of oil has been the dichotomy between the secularizing influences of modern technology and the strongly religious tradition of Saudi society. Although the two appear basically incom-patible, most Saudis have managed surprisingly well, adopting the former while clinging to the latter. There are people with extreme views, however, who can-not reconcile the two; and their positions are the most visible to the West.

Saudis who are frustrated about what they see as the slow pace of modern-ization, particularly in social development, often blame religious fanatics for being overzealous in opposing what they see as reform (including, for example, attitudes toward the role of women in society). For these Saudis, technological innovations are a gift of God to be enjoyed and appreciated as such, and social reform is not incompatible with Islam.

For those on the far religious right, modern technology is an agent of the devil to be rejected for its corrupt, secularizing influence; and social reform, which is tantamount to religious innovation, is heresy. The far religious right, however, labors under some disadvantages. It is more difficult to organize mass discontent against a regime that itself espouses Islamic values than against an avowedly secular one. Moreover, amassing wealth is not antithetical to Islam, and a doctrine of material austerity and self-denial that many militant Islam-ists believe should go along with moral asceticism would find few avid follow-ers in the kingdom's generally affluent society.

Most Saudis do not fall into either of these extremes. Highly devout people, they nevertheless have taken to technological innovation with comparative equanimity. The tension between secular modernism and religious tradition-alism, however, is likely to continue well into the future and with it the poten-tial for polarization around extremes and erosion of the center. The future direction of social development will be determined to a great extent by social trends arising from the collision of modernization and traditional culture.

Possibly the two greatest threats to social stability in the kingdom in the coming century will be urbanization and runaway population growth. Urbanization is a long-term threat to the extended family-based social system that has made Saudis so resistant to the stresses of modernization. By the year 2000, an estimated 82 percent of the population will be urban. As more and more people are located in cities and large towns, extended family ties will inevitably weaken. On the other hand, Saudi society has withstood the uprooting of nuclear families who have moved to the cities during the past forty years and has remained remarkably intact. If past trends are any guide, the family structure, while weakened, will probably continue to be one of the most stabilizing forces in the kingdom in the next century.

Population growth, running at about 3.7 percent a year, is a greater long-term threat. Moreover, the median age is dropping, meaning that an increasing number of Saudi women will be at child-bearing age for a longer period of time. In 1992, about 48 percent of the population was under fifteen years old, 58 percent under twenty, and 69 percent under twenty-five. At the present rate, the population will expand by one-third every eight years; by the year 2000 there will be 16 million Saudis, and by 2011 the population will reach 25 million, excluding expatriates.[1]

Such growth will place a tremendous strain on extended families who are seeking to maintain the loyalty and material welfare of their members. With relatively flat revenues projected over the next decade, it is not likely that the government will be able to provide the current per capita level of social and economic welfare to a rapidly expanding population, and the burden will increasingly fall on the extended families. If at some point the population is so large that the families are no longer able to meet the burden, the impact on political stability could be serious, possibly the greatest long-term threat to Saudi political security. Indeed, the impact of runaway population growth might become the greatest challenge to Saudi society, its economy, and its political system in the twenty-first century.

Prospects for Saudi Economic Development

Given Saudi Arabia's huge oil reserves and the paucity of other natural resources, it is reasonable to assume that the oil sector will continue to dominate the Saudi economy in the twenty-first century. It is also reasonable to assume that the present short-term negative cash flow problem will be solved one way or another in or by the next century. Like most major commodities, the oil market follows regular business cycles; and at some point there will almost certainly be another tight market, possibly before the end of the decade.

The current challenge facing the Saudi economy is not so much concerned with the twenty-first century as with solving the kingdom's more immediate negative cash flow problem. The prospects for raising revenues to balance the budget do not look particularly promising in the short to medium run. Another politically induced energy crisis could quickly and dramatically raise oil revenues; but such crises are too capricious to count on, and there is no guarantee that the next crisis, unlike past ones, would not include military destruction of major Saudi oil installations.

In the absence of such a crisis, oil prices are expected to rise slowly for the rest of the decade. Of course, there are many unknown factors that could change the picture for better or worse. On the supply side, for example, such factors include: whether oil production in the states of the former Soviet Union will recover faster or slower than their domestic economies, a major determinant of how much exportable oil will be available; the impact of Iraqi oil's coming back onstream, and its rate of production; the pace of long-term capital investment in oil production facilities, a major determinant in future productive capacity; and the pace of oil technology advances, also affecting future productive capacity. On the demand side, factors include the degree to which environmental and revenue-raising energy tax legislation will impede demand in the major consuming countries, and the future rate of world economic growth. Despite the uncertainties of the future oil market, it seems safe to assume that a significant rise in Saudi oil revenues will not occur until sometime in the late 1990s.

With anticipated flat oil revenues, the Saudis have had to concentrate on reducing expenditures, an extremely complex and difficult undertaking. There are several options: delaying or stretching out payments to contractors, slowing down or canceling both defense and nondefense projects, and cutting subsidies and borrowing and bartering more oil. The Saudis have used all of them. In October 1993, the government cut agricultural subsidies to wheat and barley growers by 25 percent, and King Fahd subsequently announced that the 1994 budget would be slashed 20 percent—from $52.5 billion in 1993 to $46.6 billion. The government also made public its decision to draw out planned defense expenditures beyond what was originally planned. Additional cuts in defense spending over the next several years would not be surprising.

The government has also given some thought to raising revenues through various tax schemes. Direct taxes on private and corporate income are considered politically unacceptable, but some form of indirect or hidden taxation or taxation of luxury items could be considered.

Any restructuring of comprehensive Saudi welfare programs means that some individuals and organizations will inevitably win or lose more than others, always a difficult political problem. For example, the cut in wheat and barley subsidies made economic sense because grain production was rapidly depleting underground water supplies and without subsidies Saudi wheat and barley were not competitive with overseas production. Nevertheless, with agriculture representing about 9 percent of the GDP, the cut in subsidies will create a significant decline in economic activity. Qasim province, where about half the kingdom's wheat is grown, will be particularly hard hit. It could experience as much as a 10 percent decline of its GDP if the cuts remain in effect.

In the longer run, it will be increasingly difficult to keep government expenditures down given the rapidly growing population. Costly physical and social infrastructure will have to be expanded greatly in years to come just to keep the standard of living from dropping. Schools and highways that were more than adequate a few years ago are now overcrowded in many parts of the country, and the problem is expected to get worse. Student enrollment climbed from 1.4 million in 1981 to about three million in 1989 and will soon double again. The government planned to open about eight hundred new schools and five hundred public health facilities in 1993 and had to borrow money to build them.[2] All in all, population growth is likely to be the major challenge to the Saudi economy in the twenty-first century as the government is forced to readjust its generous welfare programs, subsidies, and allowances, both budgetary and extrabudgetary, to the needs of a population that could double every twenty years.

In sum, tackling the government's negative cash flow problem is extremely difficult. So far, however, the government has demonstrated the political will to address the problem.

In contrast to the public sector, the prospects for the Saudi private sector appear somewhat brighter on the eve of the twenty-first century. With public-sector oil revenues dominating the Saudi economy, the private sector has been largely dependent on public spending and government contracts for the past generation. This, plus a traditional merchant mentality that prefers high profit margins to capital gains, retarded the development of a real entrepreneurial class in Saudi Arabia until just recently, when a new class of young Saudi venture capitalists spearheaded a domestic boom in the late 1980s and early 1990s.

The growth of this new capitalist class could have important ramifications for the future of the Saudi economy. With few natural resources other than oil and a small, relatively unproductive labor force (women are barred from most jobs, and the absence of a work ethic further limits productivity) and with private capital in relative abundance, private-sector capital investment and management may turn out to one of the most promising areas for economic development in the twenty-first century.

The relationship between a strong private sector and the government is interesting to speculate upon. Middle Eastern attitudes toward government have traditionally been negative. Historically, governments taxed citizens and drafted their sons to fight but never accepted the responsibility for their welfare. Thus, the modern Saudi welfare state is a relatively new creation, as is the dependence of Saudi citizens upon the government for its economic welfare.

With the scope of government welfare likely to decline in future years due to increased population and relatively flat revenues, the dependence of the public upon the government for general welfare could also decline and in the process might redefine the relationship between the two. A private sector less dependent on the government would probably be less interested in government operations in general but more anxious to acquire a greater voice in policy decisions that affect its own economic welfare.

Prospects for Saudi Political Development[3]

Largely because of its extraordinarily cohesive society, Saudi Arabia's political system is likely to remain stable well into the twenty-first century if population growth does not undermine it. Nevertheless, a number of major political changes and challenges will occur in the next century. One change that can be predicted with total certainty is that the current ruling generation of Al Sauds—sons of King Abd al-Aziz—will relinquish political power in the next century, if not before. Most of the senior princes are already in their seventies.

This change in leadership will have significant political implications for the kingdom. Current Saudi leaders spent their formative years in a harsh environment of poverty and hostility from enemies on every side, one that bred patience, self-reliance, and suspicion of foreigners. It was an environment closer to that of their ancestors than that of their own children. The passing of the reins of government, therefore, will be more than a simple generational change. It will mean the assumption of power by a new generation with a wholly different outlook—a generation that is Western-educated, has nearly always known affluence, and has never had to toil just to survive.

More demands will undoubtedly be placed on the new generation by a public seeking greater participation in the political process and by more complex problems, many of them defying solution or beyond the control of the government to influence in a meaningful way. Public participation in the political process is thus likely to be the key to the direction that long-term Saudi political development will take. The creation of the Majlis al-Shura by King Fahd was a creative step to institutionalize and broaden the base of public participation through the ancient medium of consultation and consensus. It is still too early to tell how the majlis will evolve, but evolve it must in the face of a rapidly modernizing society if it is to serve as a meaningful conduit for political participation.

Population growth adds an extra urgency to the problem of participation. In earlier times, a citizen could simply walk into the public majlis (the word in this context means "court" or "audience") of the king or one of his amirs to seek a favor or redress for a grievance. Now, with a much larger population and more complicated problems, government dealings with the public have perforce become far more impersonal and bureaucratized. To a society that prizes personal relationships, that is a great price to pay; and greater personal participation in the political process will almost certainly be sought as a means of compensating for the growing impersonalization of government.

Despite all the changes, the new generation of leaders will have to deal with a fairly constant set of problems in the twenty-first century: maintaining national security, both internal and external; improving the national economy, including maximizing long-term oil revenues and short-term development and welfare expenditures; diversifying the economy; and developing the society while preserving traditional Islamic values. Balancing modernization with maintaining fundamental Islamic values will continue to be a major preoccupation of the government.

Trying to predict the identity of the new generation of leaders is far more difficult than identifying the problems it will face. Among the grandsons of King Abd al-Aziz are some who are talented, well educated, and increasingly experienced technocrats; but so long as power remains in the hands of their fathers and uncles, there is no appreciable coalescence of support for any one individual or sibling group of princes.

There is, of course, no guarantee that the next generation in government will be lead by the Al Saud family. The imminent collapse of the Saudi regime has been predicted repeatedly over the years, and given enough time it may eventually come to pass. Nevertheless, short of a crisis of really gigantic proportions or some other situation that totally undermines the legitimacy of the current regime, there is little compelling reason to believe that the current regime will not remain in power into the twenty-first century.

In the event that it is replaced, the most likely successor would be a militant Islamist regime dominated by the military (the only organized group in the country with a monopoly of coercive force), which would seek to justify its claim to legitimacy through the same Wahhabi doctrine of Tawhid espoused by the Al Sauds. Such a regime, however, would probably be unstable, maintaining power by force and through calls for opposition to real and imagined enemies rather than from any positive achievements.

The least likely scenario is the creation of a secular, democratic regime modeled along Western lines. If and when Saudi Arabia ever acquires an elected, representative form of government, the political system and the political morality it is based upon are likely to reflect the teachings of Islam far more than those of Thomas Jefferson. Even among the most modernized, Western-edu-cated technocrats in the kingdom, there is virtually no desire to forsake Is-lamic political theory as the basis of the Saudi constitutional system.

From the point of view of the West, the current regime has a greater mutu-ality of interests than any likely successor. It is true that no successor, even a militantly revolutionary Islamic regime, is likely totally to abandon current Saudi oil policies. The current symbiotic relationship between Saudi Arabia and major oil-consuming states of the West is based on mutual benefit and enlightened self-interest, and Saudi Arabia and the other Gulf states have oil reserves adequate to meet the needs of the rest of the world far into the next century. Nevertheless, if the current regime were replaced by a militant one, accommodation with the West over oil policies and broader international eco-nomic issues would be virtually certain to cease. Probably the best the West could hope for in those areas would be a grudging coexistence based on the West's need to buy oil and the new regime's need to sell it.

A militant regime would also be a threat to regional stability, adopting ac-tivist foreign policies seeking to undermine the moderate regimes in neigh-boring states and elsewhere in the Muslim world. More than likely, it would also seek a nuclear arms capability to put it militarily on a par with its power-ful neighbors to the north: Israel, Iran, and Iraq. Security cooperation with the United States and the Gulf states would end, and relations with Iran, assum-ing that it still espouses Islamic revolution, would probably deteriorate fur-ther as the two regimes competed for political leadership of the Islamic world.

The advent of such a regime, however, is unlikely. Far more probable than a change of regime, or even a change of basic foreign and domestic policies, is a change of style as a new generation of Al Sauds replaces the older generation. It is likely to be far more self-assured and more independent of Western and even other Arab political pressures than the current leadership, although it would still proceed cautiously and from consensus. This could lead to a great deal more frustration in Western capitals but not so great as to undermine basically sound relationships. It is doubtful, however, that Western capitals would be able to ignore the kingdom or take it for granted to the degree they have in the past.

In sum, the most likely direction of political development in Saudi Arabia in the twenty-first century is evolutionary rather than revolutionary change. Nevertheless, when such changes are gradual and incremental, it is always a good idea periodically to test one's underlying assumptions; for conditions in this part of the world can change rapidly and without warning.

Appendix

Saudi Arabia has a closed, extended-family society, and no Saudi family is as closed to public view as the Saudi royal house, the Al Saud. As a result, royal family politics and the royal succession have generated a great deal of interest.

Figure 23 is a selected genealogy of the Al Saud, showing the succession of rulers since the founding of the dynasty and their relationships to each other. Figure 24 shows the sons of King Abd al-Aziz (Ibn Saud), the founder of modern Saudi Arabia. Since his death in 1953, the succession has passed among his sons, beginning with Saud, the eldest surviving son at the time of his death. The succession has not been determined strictly by age, however, and several sons have been passed over.

In recent years, many grandsons of King Abd al-Aziz have reached adulthood. Most are Western educated, and collectively they are the future of the dynasty. Figure 25 is a selected list of members of this generation who are or have been in public service.

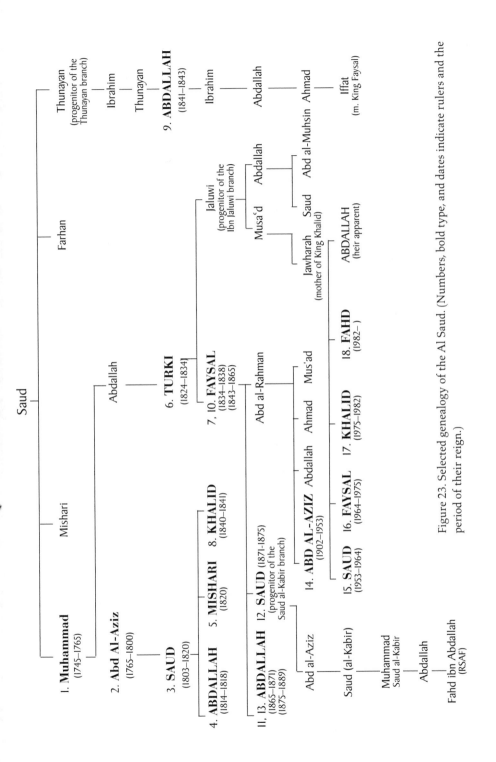

Figure 23. Selected genealogy of the Al Saud. (Numbers, bold type, and dates indicate rulers and the period of their reign.)

ABD AL-AZIZ
(r. 1902–1953)

Turki (d. 1919)	(Wadhba bint Hazzam)	(Tarfah bint Al al-Shaykh)	(Jawharah bint Musaʿd Bin Jaluwi)	(Bazza)	(Jawharah bint Saʿd al-Sudayri)	(Hussah bint al-Sudayri)
Turki (d. 1919)	**SAUD** (r. 1953–1964 d. 1969)	**FAYSAL** (r. 1964–1975)	Muhammad b. 1910	Nasir b. 1920	Saʿd b. 1920	**FAHD** b. 1920 (r. 1982–)
			KHALID b. 1912 (r. 1975–1982)	Bandar b. 1923	Musaʿid b. 1923	Sultan b. 1924
				Fawwaz b. 1934	Abd al-Muhsin b.1925	Abd al-Rahman b. 1926
						Nayif b. 1933
						Turki b. 1934
						Salman b. 1936
						Ahmad b. 1937

Figure 24. The sons of King Abd al-Aziz. (Mothers' names are in parentheses.)

continued
below

(Bint Asi al-Shuraym)	(Shahida)	(Munayir)	(Bushrah)	(Haya bint Saʿd al-Sudayri)	(Mudhi)
ABDALLAH b. 1923 (heir apparent)	Mishʿal b. 1926	Talal b. 1931	Mishari b. 1932	Badr b. 1933	Majid b. 1934
	Mitʿab b. 1928	Nawwaf b. 1934		Abd al-Ilah b. 1935	Sattam b. 1943
				Abd al-Majid b. 1940	

continued

(Bint al-Shaʿlan)	(Saʿida al-Yamaniyah)	(Barakah al-Yamaniyah)	(Futaymah al-Yamaniyah)
Thamir b. 1937	Hidhlul b. 1941	Muqrin b. 1943	Hamud b. 1947
Mamduh b. 1940			
Mashhur b. 1942			

Table: Selected grandsons of King Abd al-Aziz in public service. Fathers' names in parentheses.

(Saud)	(Faysal)	(Khalid)	(Nasir)	(Fahd)	(Abdallah)	(Sultan)	(Abd al-Muhsin)	(Nayif)	(Salman)
Sayf al-Islam *Ministry of Interior*	Saud *Foreign Minister*	Sultan *Navy Lt.*	Turki *General, Air Force*	Faysal *Director, Youth Welfare*	Mit'ib *General, National Guard*	Khalid *General, Army*	Saud *Deputy Amir, Makkah*	Fahd Ibn Turki *great-grandson* *Ministry of Interior*	Sultan *former astronaut* *Director, Agency for* *Disabled Children*
Muhammad *Amir of Baha*	Khalid *Amir of Abha*			Muhammad *Amir of Eastern Province*	Faysal *Captain,* *National Guard*	Bandar *Ambassador to the U.S.*			Abd al-Aziz *Deputy Minister* *of Petroleum*
	Bandar *Air Force*			Sultan *Deputy, Youth Welfare*		Fahd *Amir of Tabuk*			
	Turki *Director, GID*			Saud *Deputy, GID*					
				Abd al-Aziz *Royal Counselor*					

Figure 25. Selected grandsons of King Abd al-Aziz in public service. (Fathers' names are in parentheses.)

Notes

1. The Land and the People

1. "Makkah" and "al-Madinah" are the official Saudi English spellings according to the Saudi Ministry of Information.

2. For an interesting account by one of the first outsiders to traverse the area, see Thesiger, *Arabian Sands*.

3. Al-Farsy, *Modernity and Tradition*, p. 2.

4. Translation provided by George Rentz, quoted in Twitchell, *Saudi Arabia*, p. 8.

5. *New York Times*, December 16, 1992, p. A8.

6. Krimly, "The Political Economy of Rentier States," p. 332.

2. Historical Background

1. See the bibliography for books by Philby, Burton, Doughty, Ibn Bishr, and Ibn Ghanim.

2. *Shaykh* (also transliterated as *shaikh, sheikh,* and *sheik*) is an all-purpose Arabic word denoting respect. It can mean a teacher, a tribal leader, an important person, or simply a grand old man.

3. According to Philby, he belonged to the Masharifa clan of the Bani Tamim tribe. See Philby, *Arabia*, pp. 8–12.

4. Winder, *Saudi Arabia in the Nineteenth Century*, p. 228.

5. There are a number of good popular books containing biographical information on King Abd al-Aziz, including Armstrong, *Lord of Arabia;* De Gaury, *Arabia Phoenix;* Howarth, *The Desert King;* and the works of Philby cited previously. Two scholarly studies of this period are Helms, *The Cohesion of Saudi Arabia,* and Kostiner, *The Making of Saudi Arabia, 1916–1936.*

6. Philby, *Arabia*, p. 160.

7. For an analysis of the Ikhwan, see Habib, *Ibn Sa'ud's Warriors of Islam.*

8. For a description of the early constitutional and bureaucratic development of the kingdom, see Davies, "The Organization of the Government of Saudi Arabia."

9. One of the better biographies of King Faysal's early years is De Gaury, *Faysal.*

10. Author's personal notes. The ambassador was Hermann Eilts.

3. The Saudi Political System

1. "The Basic Law of Government of the Kingdom of Saudi Arabia," translated by the Foreign Broadcast Information Service, London, March 1, 1992.

2. Named after an early Islamic scholar, Ahmad Ibn Hanbal (died 855). See Esposito, *Islam*, p. 86.

3. See Coulson, *A History of Islamic Law*, pp. 83–84.

4. Fatwa of February 11, 1927, quoted in Davies, *The Organization of the Government of Saudi Arabia*, p. 33. The Arabic text is found in Wahba, *Jazirat al-'Arab fil Qarn al-'Ashrin* [The Arabian peninsula in the twentieth century].

5. Bill, "The Plasticity of Informal Politics," p. 131.

6. For a discussion of the development of humanity's subservience to the will of God, see Watt, *Free Will and Predestination in Early Islam*, pp. 135–41.

7. For a discussion of Ibn Taymiyya's views, see Nettler, "Ibn Taymiyah," in Esposito, ed., *The Oxford Encyclopedia of the Modern Islamic World*, vol. 2, pp. 165–66. His life is discussed in Williams, ed., *Islam*.

8. See Nallino, *L'Arabia Saudiana*, p. 13 ff.

9. Text of the "Royal Decree on the Regions Statute, Kingdom of Saudi Arabia," translated by the Foreign Broadcast Information Service, London, March 1, 1992.

10. *Middle East Journal* (1992), p. 496.

11. Ibid.

12. See, for example, Simon Henderson, *After King Fahd: Succession in Saudi Arabia*, Washington Institute Policy Papers, no. 37 (Washington, D.C.: Washington Institute for Near East Policy, 1994).

13. Henderson, p. 22.

4. Oil and Saudi Arabia

1. The statistics used in this chapter are based on figures I obtained from the American embassy in Riyadh; the International Energy Agency; Cambridge Energy Research Associates, Cambridge, MA; *OPEC Statistical Yearbook*, selected years; *Petroleum Economist*, selected issues; the Petroleum Finance Company, Washington; *Petroleum Intelligence Weekly*, selected issues; the Riyad Bank; and Saudi Aramco.

2. DeNovo, "The Movement for Aggressive American Oil Policy Abroad, 1918–1920," *American Historical Review*, pp. 854–76.

3. See Stocking, *Middle East Oil*. A more popularized although extensively researched account is Yergin, *The Prize*.

4. For a discussion of these events, see Stocking, *Middle East Oil*, pp. 40–65.

5. Long, *The United States and Saudi Arabia*, p. 13.

6. For an account of the founding and early days of Aramco, see Nawwab, Speers, and Hoye, eds., *Aramco and Its World*, pp. 188–97.

7. For the text of the declaration, see U.S. Department of State, *Foreign Relations of the United States, 1943*, p. 854.

8. Mikesell, *Foreign Investment in the Petroleum and Mineral Industries*, p. 220.

9. See Yergin, *The Prize*, pp. 519–27.

10. For an analysis of this period, see Richard Chadbourn Wesiberg, *The Politics of Crude Oil Pricing in the Middle East, 1970–1975.*

11. Long, *The United States and Saudi Arabia,* pp. 24–25.

12. U.S. Department of State, "The Evolution of OPEC, 1959–1983," pp. 10–11.

13. Long, *The United States and Saudi Arabia,* p. 28.

14. Based on figures from the American embassy in Riyadh and the Riyad Bank.

15. Mohammad Al-Sabban, "Additional Taxes on Oil and the Producing Countries' Response: Overreaction or Protection of Interests?" *Middle East Economic Survey,* April 26, 1993, p. D1.

5. Economic Development and Modernization

1. For an account of the creation of the banking system, see Ali, *Saudi Arabian Monetary Agency,* pp. 118–30.

2. Material in this section is drawn in part from Young, *Saudi Arabia.*

3. Royal decree 30/4/1/1046, dated 25/7/1371 (April 20, 1952), *Umm al-Qura,* 3/8/1371 (27/4/1952), cited in Ali, *Saudi Arabian Monetary Agency,* pp. 26–27.

4. Thomas W. Shea, "The Riyal: A Miracle in Money," *Aramco World* (January–February 1969), quoted in Ali, *Saudi Arabian Monetary Agency,* p. 77.

5. Statistics used in the chapter are drawn from official U.S. and Saudi government sources; the Riyad Bank; Long, *The United States and Saudi Arabia;* and Al-Farsy, *Modernity and Tradition.*

6. The Hajj

1. Grunebaum, *Muhammadan Festivals,* p. 18.

2. See Long, *The Hajj Today.*

3. For an interesting account of the Hijaz Railroad, see Ochsenwald, *The Hijaz Railroad.*

4. See *Arab News,* April 19, 1993, p. 2.

5. Long, "The Impact of the Iranian Revolution on the Arabian Peninsula and the Gulf States," pp. 108–9.

6. Meulen, *The Wells of Ibn Sa'ud,* p. 121.

7. Robert Matthew, Johnston Marshall, and Partners (RMJM), "Regional Framework, Western Regional Plan" (mimeograph, 1972), cited by T. M. Dedford, "The Hijaz Today and in 1991," U.S. Department of State, American Embassy, Jiddah, Airgram A-104, September 19, 1972, pp. 14–15.

7. Saudi Foreign and National Security Policies

1. For a fuller development of these themes, see "King Faisal's World View," chapter 10 in Beling, ed., *King Faisal and the Modernisation of Saudi Arabia,* pp. 173–83.

2. For a discussion of the classical Islamic world view, see Khadduri, *The Islamic Law of Nations.*

3. See Eddy, *F.D.R. Meets Ibn Saud.*

4. For an analysis of the GCC, see Peterson, *The Gulf Cooperation Council.*

5. For an account of Saudi military development and the U.S. role in it, see Long, *The United States and Saudi Arabia*, pp. 33–72; Cordesman, *The Gulf and the Search for Strategic Stability;* and Cordesman, *The Gulf and the West.*

6. Dekmejian, "The Rise of Political Islamism in Saudi Arabia," pp. 638–39.

7. *Washington Post,* November 14, 1995, p. A1.

8. Cordesman, "Saudi Military Forces in the 1990s," p. 53.

8. SAUDI ARABIA IN THE TWENTY-FIRST CENTURY

1. Projections, which are based on official Saudi figures, were made by David Rehfuss, former senior economist at Riyad Bank.

2. Figures provided by David Rehfuss, Riyad Bank.

3. Parts of this section are developed from Long, "Saudi Arabia in the 1990s," pp. 85–106.

SELECTED BIBLIOGRAPHY

Abir, Mordechai. *Saudi Arabia: Government, Society and the Gulf Crisis.* London: Routledge, 1993.

Ali, Mohammad Said AlHaj. *Saudi Arabian Monetary Agency: A Review of Its Accomplishments, 1372–1411 AH/1952–1991 AD.* Riyadh: Saudi Arabian Ministry of Information, Safar 1412/August 1991.

Armstrong, H. C. *Lord of Arabia.* London: Baker, 1934.

Badeeb, Saeed M. *The Saudi-Egyptian Conflict over North Yemen, 1962–1970.* Boulder, Colo.: Westview, 1986.

Baroody, George M. "The Practice of Law in Saudi Arabia." In *King Faisal and the Modernisation of Saudi Arabia,* edited by William A. Beling. London: Croom Helm; Boulder, Colo.: Westview, 1980.

Beling, William A., ed. *King Faisal and the Modernisation of Saudi Arabia.* London: Croom Helm; Boulder, Colo.: Westview, 1980.

Bill, James A. "The Plasticity of Informal Politics: The Case of Iran." *Middle East Journal* 27 (Spring 1973), pp. 131–51.

Binduqji, Husayn Hamza [Bindagji, Hussein H.]. *Jighrafia al-Mamlaka al-ʿArabiyya al-Suʿudiyya* [The geography of Saudi Arabia]. Cairo: Maktabah Anjalu Masria, 1397/1977.

Burton, Richard F. *Personal Narrative of a Pilgrimage to al-Madinah and Meccah.* 2 vols. London: Bell, 1898.

Cordesman, Anthony. *The Gulf and the Search for Strategic Stability: Saudi Arabia, the Military Balance in the Gulf, and Trends in the Arab-Israeli Military Balance.* Boulder, Colo.: Westview; London: Mansell, 1984.

———. *The Gulf and the West.* Boulder, Colo.: Westview, 1988.

———. "Saudi Military Forces in the 1990s: The Strategic Challenge of Continued Modernization." Paper delivered at "Inside Saudi Arabia: Society, Economy, and Security," a conference of the Royal Institute of International Affairs in cooperation with the Middle East Association, London, October 4–5, 1993.

Coulson, N. J. *A History of Islamic Law.* Edinburgh: University Press, 1964.

Davies, Roger. *The Organization of the Government of Saudi Arabia.* Jiddah, Saudi Arabia: American Legation, 1948.

Dawisha, Adeed I. *Saudi Arabia's Search for Security.* Adelphi Paper No. 158. London: International Institute for Strategic Studies, Winter 1979–80.

De Gaury, Gerald. *Arabia Phoenix.* London: Harrap, 1946.

———. *Faysal: King of Saudi Arabia.* New York: Praeger, 1966.

Dekmejian, R. Hrair. "The Rise of Political Islamism in Saudi Arabia." *Middle East Journal* 48 (Autumn 1994), pp. 627–43.

DeNovo, John. "The Movement for Aggressive American Oil Policy Abroad, 1918–1920." *American Historical Review* 61 (July 1956), pp. 854–76.

Doran, Charles F., and Stephen W. Buck, eds. *The Gulf, Energy, and Global Security: Political and Economic Issues.* Boulder, Colo.: Rienner, 1991.

Doughty, Charles M. *Travels in Arabia Deserta.* Cambridge: Cambridge University Press, 1888.

Eddy, William. *F.D.R. Meets Ibn Saud.* New York: American Friends of the Middle East, 1954.

Esposito, John L., ed. *The Iranian Revolution: Its Global Impact.* Miami: Florida International Press, 1990.

———. *Islam: The Straight Path.* New York: Oxford University Press, 1988.

———, ed. *The Oxford Encyclopedia of the Modern Islamic World.* 4 vols. New York: Oxford University Press, 1995.

———, ed. *Voices of Resurgent Islam.* New York: Oxford University Press, 1983.

Al-Farsy, Fouad. *Modernity and Tradition: The Saudi Equation.* London: Kegan Paul International, 1990.

Gauze, F. Gregory. *Saudi-Yemeni Relations: Domestic Structures and Foreign Influence.* New York: Columbia University Press, 1990.

Grunebaum, Gustav E. Von. *Muhammadan Festivals.* New York: Henry Schuman, 1951.

Ibn Bishr, 'Uthman. *'Unwan al-Majd fi Tarikh Najd* [Chapters of the glory in the history of Najd]. Riyadh: Dar Banna lil Tiba'a wa Tajlid, 1953.

Ibn Ghanim, Husayn. *Rawdhat al-Afkar wal Afham: Tarikh Najd* [A garden of meditations and understandings: the history of Najd]. Riyadh: al-Maktabah al-Ahliyyah, 1949.

Ibn Taymiyyah, Taqi al-Din Ahmad. *Al-Siyasa al-Shari'iyyah* [Islamic politics]. Beirut: Dar al-Kutub al-'Arabiyyah, 1966.

Habib, John S. *Ibn Saud's Warriors of Islam: The Ikhwan and Their Role in the Creation of the Sa'udi Kingdom, 1910–1930.* Leiden: Brill, 1978.

Hamza, Fuad. *Al-Bilad al-'Arabiyya al-Su'udiyya* [The country of Saudi Arabia]. Riyadh: Maktabah al-Nasr al-Haditha, 1968.

Helms, Christine Moss. *The Cohesion of Saudi Arabia.* London: Croom Helm; Baltimore: Johns Hopkins University Press, 1981.

Henderson, Simon. *After King Fahd: Succession in Saudi Arabia.* Washington Institute Policy Paper No. 37. Washington, D.C.: Washington Institute for Near East Policy, 1994.

Holden, David. *Farewell to Arabia.* London: Faber, 1966.

Howarth, David. *The Desert King: Ibn Saud and His Arabia.* New York: McGraw-Hill, 1964.

Howarth, David, and Richard Johns. *The House of Saud.* London: Sidgwick and Jackson, 1981.

Huyette, Summer Scott. *Political Adaptation in Sa'udi Arabia.* Boulder, Colo.: Westview, 1985.

Johany, Ali D. *The Myth of the OPEC Cartel: The Role of Saudi Arabia.* New York: Wiley, 1982.

Khadduri, Majid. *The Islamic Law of Nations: Shaybani's Siyar.* Baltimore: Johns Hopkins University Press, 1966.

Kostiner, Joseph. *The Making of Saudi Arabia, 1916–1936: From Chieftancy to Monarchical State.* New York: Oxford University Press, 1994.

Krimly, Rayed Khalid. "The Political Economy of Rentier States: A Case Study of Saudi Arabia in the Oil Era." Ph.D. diss., George Washington University, 1993.

Lacey, Robert. *The Kingdom.* London: Hutcheson, 1981.

Lees, Bryan. *A Handbook of the Al Saʿud Ruling Family of Saʿudi Arabia.* London: Royal Genealogies, 1980.

Long, David E. *The Hajj Today: A Survey of the Contemporary Pilgrimage to Makkah.* Albany: State University of New York Press, 1979.

———. "The Impact of the Iranian Revolution on the Arabian Peninsula and the Gulf States." In *The Iranian Revolution: Its Global Impact,* edited by John L. Esposito. Miami: Florida International University Press, 1990.

———. "King Faisal's World View." In *King Faisal and the Modernisation of Saudi Arabia,* edited by Willard A. Beling. London: Croom Helm; Boulder, Colo.: Westview, 1980.

———. *Saudi Arabia.* Washington Papers 4, no. 39. Beverly Hills, Calif. and London: Sage, 1976.

———. "Saudi Arabia in the 1990s: Plus Ça Change." In *The Gulf, Energy and Global Security: Political and Economic Issues,* edited by Charles F. Doran and Stephen W. Buck. Boulder, Colo.: Rienner, 1991.

———. "Saudi Arabia and Its Neighbors: Preoccupied Paternalism." In *Crosscurrents in the Gulf,* edited by Richard Sindelar and J. E. Peterson for the Middle East Institute. London: Routledge, 1988.

———. "Saudi Foreign Policy and the Arab-Israeli Peace Process: The Fahd (Arab) Peace Plan." In *Middle East Peace Plans,* edited by Willard A. Beling. London: Croom Helm, 1986.

———. *The United States and Saudi Arabia: Ambivalent Allies.* Boulder, Colo.: Westview, 1985.

Mikesell, Raymond F., ed. *Foreign Investment in the Petroleum and Mineral Industries.* Baltimore: Johns Hopkins University Press, 1971.

Meulen, D. Van der. *The Wells of Ibn Saʿud.* New York: Praeger, 1957.

Nallino, Carlo Alfonso. *L'Arabia Saudiana.* Vol. 1 of *Raccolta di scritti editi e inediti,* edited by Maria Nallino. Rome: Istituto per l'Oriente, 1939.

Nawwab, Ismail, Peter Speers, and Paul F. Hoye, eds. *Aramco and Its World: Arabia and the Middle East.* Washington: Arabian American Oil Company, 1980.

Nyang, Sulayman, and Evan Hendricks. *A Line in the Sand: Saudi Arabia's Role in the Gulf War.* Washington: P.T. Books, 1995.

Ochsenwald, William. *Religion, Society and the State in Arabia: The Hijaz under Ottoman Control, 1849–1908.* Columbus: Ohio State University Press, 1984.

———. *The Hijaz Railroad.* Charlottesville: University of Virginia Press, 1980.

Painter, David S. *Oil and the American Century.* Baltimore: Johns Hopkins University Press, 1986.

Peters, F. E. *The Hajj: The Muslim Pilgrimage to Mecca and the Holy Places.* Princeton, N.J.: Princeton University Press, 1994.

Peterson, Erik R. *The Gulf Cooperation Council: Search for Unity in a Dynamic Region.* Boulder, Colo.: Westview, 1988.

Philby, H. St. John B. *Arabia.* London: Benn, 1930.

———. *Arabia of the Wahhabis.* London: Constable, 1928.

———. *Arabian Days: An Autobiography.* London: Hale, 1948.

———. *Arabian Jubilee.* London: Hale, 1952.

———. *Arabian Oil Ventures.* Washington: Middle East Institute, 1964.

———. *Sa'udi Arabia.* New York: Arno, 1972.

Rihani, Amin. *Ibn Sa'oud of Arabia.* London: Constable, 1928.

Shaw, John A., and David E. Long. *Saudi Arabian Modernization: The Impact of Change on Stability.* Washington Papers 10, no. 89. New York: Praeger, 1982.

Stocking, George W. *Middle East Oil: A Study in Political and Economic Controversy.* Nashville, Tenn.: Vanderbilt University Press, 1970.

Sultan, Khaled bin, with Patrick Seale. *Desert Warrior: A Personal View of the Gulf War by the Joint Forces Commander.* New York: HarperCollins, 1995.

Thesiger, Wilfred. *Arabian Sands.* London: Readers Union/Longman, 1960.

Twitchell, Karl S. *Saudi Arabia: With an Account of the Development of Its Natural Resources.* 3d ed. New York: Greenwood, 1958.

U.S. Department of State, Office of the Historian. "The Evolution of OPEC, 1959–1983." Historical Research Project No. 1349 (undated).

U.S. Department of State. *Foreign Relations of the United States, 1943.* Vol. 4. Washington: Government Printing Office.

Wahba, Hafiz. *Arabian Days.* London: Barker, 1964.

———. *Jazira al-'Arab fi al-Qarn al-'Ashrin* [The Arabian peninsula in the twentieth century]. Cairo: Matba'ah al-Nahdah al-Misriyyah, 1961.

Watt, W. Montgomery. *Free Will and Predestination in Early Islam.* London: Luzac, 1948.

Weisberg, Richard Chadbourn. *The Politics of Crude Oil Pricing in the Middle East, 1970–1975: A Study in International Bargaining.* Series No. 31. Berkeley, Calif.: Institute of International Studies, University of California, 1977.

Williams, John Alden, ed. *Islam.* New York: Braziller, 1961.

Winder, R. Bayly. *Saudi Arabia in the Nineteenth Century.* New York: St. Martin's, 1965.

Al-Yassini, Ayman. *Religion and State in the Kingdom of Saudi Arabia.* Boulder, Colo.: Westview, 1985.

Yergin, Daniel. *The Prize: The Epic Quest for Oil, Money and Power.* New York: Simon and Schuster, 1990.

Young, Arthur N. *Saudi Arabia: The Making of a Financial Giant.* New York: New York University Press, 1983.

INDEX